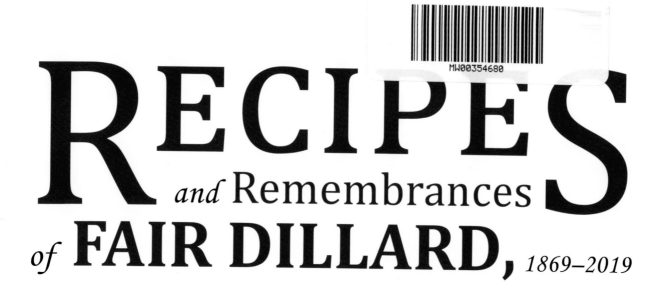

RECIPES
and Remembrances
of FAIR DILLARD, *1869–2019*

RECIPES
and Remembrances
of FAIR DILLARD, *1869–2019*

ZELLA PALMER

2019
UNIVERSITY OF LOUISIANA AT LAFAYETTE PRESS

Special thanks to Dr. Walter M. Kimbrough, Mrs. Adria Kimbrough, President of the Ray Charles Foundation Valerie Ervin, and Ms. Sybil Haydel-Morial. Also, Dillard University Vice-President of Institutional Development, Marc Barnes; Vice-President of Academic Affairs, Dr. Yolanda W. Page; Director of Community Relations, Nick Harris; Dean of Faculty, Dr. Eartha Johnson; Director of the Dillard University Library, Cynthia Charles; Dillard University Will W. Alexander Library Staff: Archives and Special Collections Librarian, Beverly Harris; Archives and Special Collections Assistant, John Kennedy; Access Services Assistant; Student Workers Supervisor, Malik Bartholomew; Event Planner and Auxiliary Services, Michelle Mathews; Amistad Research Center, Dr. Kara T. Olidge, and Long Vue House and Gardens.

And finally, thank you readers. Proceeds from the sale of this book will benefit Dillard University.

http://ulpress.org
University of Louisiana at Lafayette Press
P.O. Box 43558
Lafayette, LA 70504-3558

Printed on acid-free paper in Canada
Library of Congress Cataloging-in-Publication Data

Names: Palmer, Zella, author.
Title: Recipes and Remembrances of Fair Dillard : 1869-2019 / Zella Palmer.
Description: Lafayette, LA : University of Louisiana at Lafayette Press, 2019.
Identifiers: LCCN 2018051548 | ISBN 9781946160478 (acid-free paper)
Subjects: LCSH: International cooking. | Cooking--Louisiana. | Dillard
  University. | LCGFT: Community cookbooks.
Classification: LCC TX725.A1 P25 2019 | DDC 641.59763--dc23
LC record available at https://lccn.loc.gov/2018051548

Dedicated to Dillard University
and
Leah Lange Chase (1923–2019)

CONTENTS

PREFACE by Dr. Walter M. Kimbrough XI

FOREWORD by Leah Chase XIII

INTRODUCTION by Zella Palmer 1

THE DILLARD WOMEN'S CLUB COOKBOOK:
A COLLECTION OF FINE RECIPES INCLUDING LOUISIANA CUISINE, FOREIGN DISHES, AND FAVORITE FAMILY RECIPES

Introduction by Sybil Haydel Morial 13

A Few Favorite Recipes from a Few Favorite Friends............................ 19
Around the World Recipes.. 37
Creole Recipes 49
Louisiana Yams Around the Clock: Pies, Cakes, Vegetables, Etc. 63
Appetizers, Pickles, and Relish 69
Soup, Salads, Sauces, Dressings 73
Main Dishes—Meat, Seafood, Poultry 81
Main Dishes—Cheese, Egg, Spaghetti, Casserole 92
Vegetables 97
Bread, Rolls, Pies, and Pastry... 105
Cakes, Cookies, and Icings 113
Desserts.. 122

DILLARD AUXILIARY'S INTERNATIONAL FOOD FESTIVAL COOKBOOK:
PRESIDENT SAMUEL DuBOIS COOK, 1973–1997
"THE DILLARD UNIVERSITY EXPERIENCE IS GLOBAL"

Letter from Dillard University President Samuel DuBois Cook 127

African... 131
American 134
Asian-American 135
Creole/Cajun 136
Soul 141
Southwestern 144
European 147
Breads, Pastries, Cakes 150

Fair Dillard: A Collection of Contemporary Recipes
President Walter M. Kimbrough, 2012–

Introduction by Mrs. Adria Nobles Kimbrough 159

New Orleans 161
American 183
Southern 185
International 188
Vegetarian 196
Desserts 199
Beverages 206

ENDNOTES 211
IMAGE CREDITS 213
RECIPE INDEX 215

Hello!

ONE OF THE SIGNATURE CATCHPHRASES of the late musical icon Ray Charles was one word—"Hello!" While generally used as a greeting, Charles and many African-Americans have used it as a statement of agreement of affirmation. It has to be said with a kind of attitude for best effect.

Dillard University's Ray Charles Program in African-American Material Culture was officially launched in 1998 with a gift from the Ray Charles Foundation in Los Angeles. It was a recognition of Dillard University's history of engaging the community. Under the leadership of current chair Zella Palmer and with continued generous support by the Ray Charles Foundation, the program has been a strong presence in New Orleans.

Today, the program hosts a number of educational and cultural events on campus, partnering with local and national groups and experts to explore the food culture of New Orleans. Ray Charles was, like most of us, enamored with food in New Orleans. The Ray Charles program allows us to learn more about this culture so that its history and traditions are not lost.

This cookbook revives a Dillard tradition, as these kinds of cookbooks have been produced in previous eras. Under the administrations of previous Dillard presidents Albert W. Dent (1941–1969) and Samuel DuBois Cook (1974–1997), the university produced cookbooks that looked deep into the community for recipes. This cookbook is thus a historical document as well as a way to pass down African-American food culture to the next generation. Thank you to all of the contributors to the project.

I hope that you will enjoy trying these recipes and sharing the dishes with your family and friends. And when you have those first bites, maybe you will remember Ray and signify your approval with the food by uttering a simple, one-word affirmation—Hello!

Dr. Walter M. Kimbrough

FOREWORD

LEAH CHASE

JESSIE DENT WAS DYNAMITE.
Jessie Dent was a class act. Jessie Dent was a powerhouse and mover and shaker. She was elegant, knowledgeable. She knew what they ate.

She was before her time. She was a talented piano player. Her mother was interesting too.

In those days, you couldn't go to hotels or restaurants in the French Quarter during segregation unless you worked there. When the famous opera singer Marian Anderson came to New Orleans, she stayed with Jessie Dent's mother. When she came in the 1940s, I was working in the French Quarter.

Jessie Dent knew how to teach them. She was a good leader. She started so many good things. She was able to get Eunice Johnson to bring *Ebony* Fashion Fair to New Orleans in the 1950s. The money raised helped Flint-Goodridge Hospital. They asked me to help raise money for Flint-Goodridge Hospital. My job was selling pies and suppers. Everyone had their part to play. We just did what needed to be done.

Flint-Goodridge
Hospital waiting room

We didn't have many outlets but we had our HBCUs. Jessie Dent knew how to entertain and build alliances—from the silver to the dishes she served. We have come a long way.

African-Americans had those things, they just didn't pay attention to it. We had so much going for us but we didn't realize it. We had master cooks, master plasterers, seamstresses that did masterful work. In our eyes, we were just doing our job.

African-Americans had businesses but we didn't know much about how to run a business. We were never taught how to run a business. We just did it. It's amazing how they taught themselves. We had our own life insurance, banks, and funeral homes. Our own society. They would say, "I am going to pay my society." Every Sunday they paid into their life insurance policies. Those banks, funeral directors, and HBCU presidents were our leaders. No banks would loan us money because they knew what we would do for our communities. It was so natural for them to keep us down.

Back in those days, I had no education. I wasn't part of the Dillard society. Dillard was considered our Ivy League school. They were considered society people. They were trying to uplift themselves. It was a hard time, we had to lift ourselves up. You did the best you could. Many of my grandchildren graduated from Dillard University. Their nursing school was stellar. They turned out so many good nurses. They are needed today more than ever. Dr. Dent built Flint-Goodridge Hospital. That was a huge achievement.

By the 1960s, people started coming together. Dillard was all about uplift-ment. It took a turn in the 1960s. We started to look at the value of each other more. We had to do it together. We had to use all of the resources we had. Dr. Albert and Jessie Dent knew that. I loved their son, Tom Dent, too. I would wait for him. He liked fried oysters and grits. I prepared it for him. He was brilliant. He did so much to uplift people so they could grow.

Samuel DuBois Cook was younger and had more ideas as Dillard University president. He saw a broader picture. He was another dynamite person. He brought the President of Duke University, Terry Sanford. He educated people. Every president came with their own ideas and built on it. His wife, Sylvia Cook, did things in her own way. Dr. Cook brought people to Dooky Chase. I would ask him, "What do you want me to prepare?" I would try to get him to eat something different but he would say, "No Leah, I like seafood plates with stuffed crabs and a side of onion rings."

Another supporter of Dillard University was Justice Revius Ortique; he brought everyone to Dooky Chase. He loved fried catfish, potato salad, and sweet potatoes.

Food is so important. If I know what you like to eat, it tells me a lot about you, and this cookbook tells a lot about Dillard University and New Orleans. We do everything with food in New Orleans. You can tell so many stories through a cookbook. They are so important.

I remember being just a poor country girl listening to the radio in Madison-ville, Louisiana, and ironing my clothes and hearing Mussolini speak. It was hard times worldwide, and we all listened to the radio. And then there is this little man with so much power named Emperor Haile Selassie from Ethiopia. He came to New Orleans with his daughter. I heard he was coming to New Orleans and would parade down Canal Street. I dressed my kids up to take them to Canal Street. I was so sad. Nobody on the street stopped. I remember standing there with my children that were so excited to see him. He was a little giant in my eyes. I never forgot that. I knew then that I had to educate my children, so they knew who their people were. We were ashamed to talk about things.

I remember Eleanor Roosevelt. She went to bat for many African-Americans. She stood her ground even if she received backlash. When I think of it now and reflect that the Roosevelts came to New Orleans and to Dillard University. It's unbelievable. Edgar and Edith Stern also believed differently and helped Dillard and African-Americans out a lot. They are still respected in our community. And then I think about the people who came to my restaurant, and I am just so thankful.

You have to give people the best you have. I was in high school at St. Mary's Academy when the nuns took us to see President Franklin Roosevelt. I never thought as a young girl that one day I would serve three American presidents, Bill Clinton, George Bush, and Barack Obama, and then the President of Mexico and Prime Minister of Canada.

I want readers to know when they read this cookbook how people lived back then, right or wrong. We had to live with each other to succeed. What powerhouses and resources they lost by keeping us back. Had you educated them, things would have been a lot different, but they couldn't see that. So we just rose above it and kept going. Those that had the education and money still couldn't spend and go where they wanted. It is important for people to see how far we have come. Black men were beaten and black women had to go out and work and take care of the children. These stories were never told. The youth, both black and white, need to know this.

Leah Chase
September 19, 2018
Dooky Chase Restaurant

Author Zella Palmer and Leah Chase

INTRODUCTION

ZELLA PALMER

NEW ORLEANS. 1935. After careful consideration, the Dillard University editorial staff agreed on a name for their inaugural student-run magazine. They named it *Courtbouillon*. In the first editorial letter, entitled "What's in a Name," the students explained their rationale for naming the student magazine. They began by reflecting on the history of New Orleans and by describing the "old city as crinoline, old lace, candlelight and above all else, of old wine and rare foods." They extolled one of the city's chief glories—Creole cookery and the classic dish that had once been a favorite in New Orleans, courtbouillon, a stew of fish, onions, thyme, parsley, and other seasoning ingredients derived from French cookery, yet accented by strong West African and Caribbean notes. In the first issue, the students said their magazine would embody the essence of the classic dish, and they promised "to stir, to strain, and to 'cook up' a delectable morsel for (our) readers." [1]

That same year, Dillard University opened its doors for the first time in the historic Gentilly neighborhood as a historically black liberal arts college, built on Christian principles of values and excellence, after a merger between Straight College and New Orleans University, which had been in existence since 1869.

In 1941, Dr. Albert W. Dent, a Morehouse College graduate who had a distinguished career as a hospital and university administrator, was appointed the second president of Dillard University. With his wife Ernestine Jessie Covington Dent, a graduate of Oberlin Conservatory of Music, fellow of the Juilliard Musical Foundation, and noted concert

Portrait of Straight University Class of 1896

1

pianist and humanitarian, they established a climate at Dillard over the next twenty-eight years of gracious hospitality and support for the arts, the student body, and campus development. Among some of the prominent speakers invited to campus and their home included Ethiopian Emperor Haile Selassie, First Lady Eleanor Roosevelt, opera diva Marian Anderson, and educator Dr. Mary McLeod Bethune.

Below, top: Dillard President Dent and Mrs. Eleanor Roosevelt at WDSU studio, 1953

Below, bottom: Mr. Stern, Emperor Haile Selassie I, Albert W. Dent, Mayor DeLesseps Story Morrison

One of the most prominent guests of the Dents was "a descendant of the oldest and longest line of royalty recorded in history,"[2] Ethiopian Emperor Haile Selassie. During his tour of the United States, Selassie arrived in New Orleans on June 25, 1954, weeks after the passing of the United States Supreme Court ruling on *Brown vs. Board of Education*. When he arrived, the city of New Orleans displayed a level of racial tolerance that had never been seen before in the segregated South. Although many whites in New Orleans disapproved of the Emperor's visit and having to make amendments for the Emperor and his party, they were nonetheless celebrated as highly esteemed dignitaries.

Emperor Selassie's motorcade was greeted by thousands of New Orleanians, both black and white. Interviewed in French by local newspapers and quoted as feeling "*tres content*" with New Orleans, he was moved with enthusiasm and interest in the "most unique" city in America, and he was anxious to experience New Orleans's fried chicken, shrimp, and hot jazz.[3]

Selassie's only public speech was given at Dillard University to nearly 3,000 people, both black and white, when President Dent announced to the large audience and to a live radio broadcast the appointment of Emperor Haile Selassie to the Dillard University Board of Trustees. Emperor Selassie humbly accepted the appointment then spoke boldly about his strong belief in full equality for all mankind.

The principles of the Christian Religion and, indeed, of good government everywhere require the observance of equality in human relations. By equality, we mean the right for all people to make their respective contributions to the progress and development of the society in which they are called upon to live. It is recognizing this principle that it will be possible to solve the problems provoking much of the unrest in the world today.[4]

Left: The banquet honoring Haile Selassie at the International House, June 24, 1954. Third from left, Haile Selassie, and fourth from left, Mrs. deLesseps Morrison

Below: Photograph from banquet honoring Haile Selassie

The royal party and New Orleans city officials attended a formal reception at President Dent's home, where "scores of the city's principal white business leaders mixed with prominent local Negroes honored Haile Selassie."[5] The state dinner was held at the International House on Camp Street. The emperor and his royal entourage were toasted with champagne, presented with a *café brulot* set, and they dined on some of the finest New Orleans cuisine. Emperor Haile Selassie was surrounded by African-Americans who were "thrilled to see HIM."[6]

There were more than 500 couples milling around inside the swank International House, where generally the only spot of color is provided by waiters and maids. The Emperor and family flanked by the high city officials, stood in semi-circle in the reception room and graciously touched the proffered hands of the city's social elite. Toasts of champagne were drunk in the Emperor's honor and white coated waiters passed through the assemblage with an endless flow of cooling liquids. Not since the visit of the King and Queen of Greece had there been anything to match this social outpouring.[7]

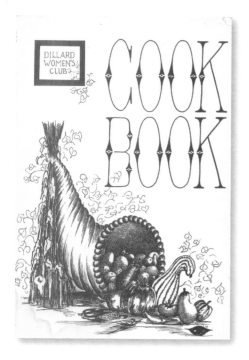

Above: Cover for the *The Dillard Women's Club Cookbook*

Below: Alpha Kappa Alpha - Alpha Beta Omega chapter with Marian Anderson, 1941

To showcase the extraordinary relationships that the Dents cultivated, Mrs. Dent led the Dillard Women's Club to publish its first cookbook in 1958 to raise funds for student scholarships. *The Dillard Women's Club Cookbook: A Collection of Fine Recipes including Louisiana Cuisine, Foreign Dishes, and Favorite Family Recipes* was an intimate cookbook filled with recipes from eminent associates, notable university faculty, and New Orleans's black elite. The cookbook gives readers a glimpse into the extensive respect the university attracted.

Eleanor Roosevelt contributed the first recipe, a Huckleberry Dessert.[8] Mrs. Roosevelt was a staunch advocate for education and ally of many African-American leaders and causes. Roosevelt recalled in her journal a 1953 visit to the Dents' home for a private lunch with Dillard faculty. Roosevelt was also invited to a private dinner at the picturesque estate of New Orleans philanthropist and Dillard University prime supporter Edgar Bloom Stern and his wife Edith Rosenwald Stern, daughter of Julius Rosenwald of Sears, Roebuck, and Company.

Other notables also submitted their favorite recipes. Opera singers Marian Anderson and Leontyne Price: South American Pudding and Champignons au Vin (Mushrooms in Wine); Dr. Mary McLeod Bethune, advisor to President Franklin D. Roosevelt and First Lady Eleanor Roosevelt and founder of the National Council of Negro Women: Old Fashioned Brown Sugar Cookies; Nobel Peace Prize Winner, Ralph J. Bunche: Creamed Sweetbreads; *Ebony Magazine* Food Editor Freda De Knight: Spiced Chicken Legs (in Black Cherries and Wine); Straight College graduate and pioneering black dermatologist Dr. Theodore K. Lawless: Ginger Bread-Hot Cakes of Honolulu; Hollywood and Broadway actresses, Etta Moten and Lena Horne: Indonesian Chicken (African Groundnut Stew) and East Indian Chicken; and New Orleans education advocate and Straight College graduate Fannie C. Williams: Plain Muffins.

The chapter "Around the World" included recipes from the Israeli Embassy: Chatazilm (Eggplant Aubergine); and from Mrs. Louise Yancy, the daughter-in-law of former Liberian Vice President Allen N. Yancy: Liberian Perlieu Rice.

Indicative of the time period, the cookbook includes lagniappe sections for the woman who entertains at home, with etiquette guides, proper table settings, dietary suggestions, calorie charts, kitchen ideas, and spot removal tips.

The chapters "Creole Recipes"; "Louisiana Yams Around the Clock: Pies, Cakes, Vegetables, Etc."; "Soup, Salads, Sauces, and Dressings"; "Main Dishes: Meat, Seafood, Poultry, and Favorite Family Recipes" include lost New Orleans Creole dishes such as Calas, Courtbouillon a la Creole, Oysters a la Poulette, Cawain, and Grillades.

The cookbook was subsidized by paid advertisements from local New Orleans businesses such as Luzianne Coffee, Langlois Candy Company, Wholesale Grocers Gerde, Newman & Company, Bagille's Seafood Company, Hubigs Pies, and Pepsi Cola Bottling Company. The Louisiana Sweet Potato Commission also provided recipes for the "Louisiana Yams Around the Clock" section.

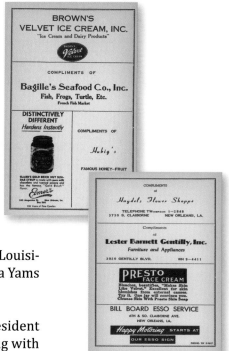

Advertisements from local New Orleans businesses in the Dillard Women's Club Cookbook

With finesse and effective strategic planning, Dillard University President Dent guided Dillard University for twenty-eight years while grappling with segregated New Orleans, World War II, the civil rights movement, and the Black Power movement. President Dent's obituary in the February 13, 1984, *New York Times* called him "a community leader and a prime mover in improving race relations through his quiet lobbying and his access to white leaders."[9]

The Dents' first son, Thomas Covington Dent, grew up watching his remarkable parents host the forefathers of the civil rights and African Independence movements in their home and on Dillard's campus. Tom Dent left his prestigious parents' home to pursue a BA in Political Science from Morehouse College (1952) and to do graduate work at Syracuse University's School of International Studies (1952–1956). After serving two years in the United States Army, Tom Dent moved to New York City in 1959, where he developed his own activist voice while working as a press attaché and public information director with the NAACP Legal Defense Fund under Thurgood Marshall.

In 1962, Tom Dent became one of the founding members of the Umbra Writer's Workshop which, while short lived, produced well-known voices of the Black Arts Movement, such as Amira Baraka, Kalamu ya Salaam, Ishmael Reed, and Askia Touré. By 1968, Dent had returned to New Orleans to promote the Free Southern Theatre, a community theatre in the Lower Ninth Ward on Louisa Street that encouraged southern black theatre performances and literary development.

BLKARTSOUTH evolved from the Free Southern Theatre in 1968, co-founded by Tom Dent and former Umbra Writer's Workshop writer and New Orleans native, Kalamu ya Salaam. Together they published their first journal, *Echoes from the Gumbo*, to reflect the multi-faceted New Orleans culture rooted in African cultural memories. After researching the origin of "gumbo," Salaam and Dent changed the journal's name to *Nkombo*, the African Bantu word for gumbo. *Nkombo* was influenced by the legend of the maroon colonies of runaway slaves who escaped to the Louisiana marshlands and developed their own community independent of the brutal slavery system.

> *The Maroons were constantly on the move. The Spanish were always after them. They had to hunt for their food and make a basic gumbo with what was available to them in order to survive: crabs, crawfish, shrimp, okra and filé was used as a preservative. There was no refrigeration. They had to sassafras it so that it would be good the next day. Reminiscent of the Maroons, our writing represented different tastes and ingredients but it was all in the same pot.* [10]

In order to raise funds to support BLKARTSOUTH, organizers would host Friday fish frys when trout were plentiful in New Orleans. On Saturday evenings, in partnership with the New Orleans NAACP, BLKARTSOUTH would sell suppers and beer. These fundraising events helped to launch community programs such as a pre-k to third grade theater program in the Lower Ninth Ward at the Ahidiana Work Study Center. BLKARTSOUTH also provided healthy meals and maintained a vegetable garden for the students.

Aerial view of Dillard, December 1961

We had this whole vegetarian approach after we started researching food preparation. I didn't know about lentils and couscous. We didn't grow up eating that kind of food. If you were active in anyway politically, you knew you had to eat to live. [11]

In 1968, Tom Dent and a Dillard University student organization, African Americans for Progress founded and organized the Festival of Afro-American Arts on campus. The Festival of Afro-American Arts is rumored to have inspired the famous New Orleans Jazz and Heritage Festival, founded in 1970.[12] The Festival of Afro-American Arts hosted national figures and local artists, such as poet Sonia Sanchez, jazz singer Abbey Lincoln, and local talent such as the Desire Community Choir, Danny Barker, Earl Turbinton, and the Dashiki Project Theatre. Although the Festival of Afro-American Arts was short-lived, the core members of the African Americans for Progress, David Dennis, Karl Baloney, and Don Hubbard, meet yearly for lunch at Dooky Chase Restaurant in New Orleans's Tremé neighborhood.

Samuel DuBois Cook was inaugurated as Dillard University's fourth president in 1974. Cook was known as the "foodie" president. On many occasions, President Cook fed the entire Dillard University student body at university picnics, cookouts, and luncheons. His beloved wife, Sylvia F. Cook, in the spirit of her predecessor Jessie Covington Dent, led the university in launching the International Food Festival. Prominent Dillard faculty members Dr. Jaqueline G. Houston and Dr. Keith Wismar compiled and edited the companion book, *The Dillard University Auxiliary International Food Festival Cookbook*, which magnified the auspicious place of Dillard University in New Orleans, the unofficial culinary capital of the United States.

Dr. Samuel DuBois Cook

President Cook's foreword captures the spirit of the university and the prominent role foodways played on campus.

> *Dillard is a very special place. It is a place of excitement, meaning, dynamic interactions, creative encounters, and joy. It harbors and begets the richness of diversity, individuality, and the common life....This cookbook contains the recipes of exotic cuisine and dishes from around the world: African, Creole, Oriental, Cajun, "Soul," French Southwestern United States, German, Spanish, Caribbean, South American, etc. All kinds of succulent specialties are included. What a treat, challenge, and opportunity. Cooking is a great art. And a great "fine art" at that. To learn and master delicate new recipes is a special artistic experience and source of enjoyment and expanded self-esteem and self-confidence.*[13]

The cookbook is a memento to faculty and staff who served "Fair Dillard" and a testament to the breadth and scope of Dillard's foodways. Recipes include Nigerian Moi Moi and Jollof Rice; New Orleans Crawfish Bisque, Red Beans and Rice, Jambalaya, and Gumbo; a variety of American Chili recipes; Assistant Professor of English, Helen Malin's Lussekatter (Swedish letter buns); The Million Dollar Chocolate Cake from Dr. Jacqueline Houston's mother; and a special contribution from Mrs. Daisy Young, a native of New Orleans fondly known as "Gram," who submitted her son, former Atlanta Mayor and UN Ambassador, Andrew Young's favorite dishes—Deviled Crabs and Ground Beef Casserole.

DILLARD AUXILIARY'S
International
Food Festival
COOKBOOK
Premier Edition

In 2003, near the end of his tenure as Dillard's fifth president, Dr. Michael L. Lomax met with the legendary musician and philanthropist Ray Charles to create the first professorship in African-American culinary history in the country and to develop an institution to preserve African American material culture in New Orleans and the South.

Marc Barnes, Dillard University Vice-President of Institutional Advancement, recalled the historic meeting between Dr. Lomax and Ray Charles:

> We met Ray Charles on Dillard's campus and had dinner with him at Dr. Lomax's house. Mr. Charles mentioned to those attending the meeting how much he loved New Orleans and its cuisine. Ray Charles spent a lot of time in New Orleans. He was extremely concerned that the food culture in New Orleans was going to be extinct now that families were busier, meals were microwaved, youth were not taught to cook like they used to, and recipes were not passed down. He really saw it as a dying art and it bothered him to the core. Mr. Charles wanted to put together an institution that would not only preserve our food but New Orleans culture so that younger generations would know how important New Orleans cooking and culture is to our city and to the world.[14]

In May of 2003, Ray Charles was awarded an honorary degree from Dillard University. Six months later, Charles donated one million dollars to Dillard University; sadly, a year later, Ray Charles died.

The September 2014 issue of *Dillard Today* magazine interviewed the "Queen of New Orleans Creole Cuisine" Leah Chase and her husband Edgar "Dooky" Chase Jr. about their more than fifty-year friendship with Ray Charles and his love for food. "He liked down home cooking. Red beans and rice and stewed chicken were his favorite. He was trained to pay back. He felt that the food he grew up with would be gone if he didn't do something to preserve it. I think he appreciated the honor he was given at Dillard and this was his way of giving back." Leah Chase now serves as the Dillard University Ray Charles Culinary Ambassador.[15]

In 2005, Hurricane Katrina hit Dillard University hard, with a total damage of $348 million. Newly inaugurated Dillard President Dr. Marvalene Hughes, faced with overwhelming challenges, worked diligently with Dillard faculty and staff, the community, private donors, and the government to restore and rebuild the serene historic campus and its student bodies. The Ray Charles Program in African-American Material Culture was dormant during the rebuilding of Dillard University post-Katrina, but it was revived when pioneering culinary historian and author Dr. Jessica B. Harris was appointed as the inaugural chair in 2009 until 2012. Dr. Harris made significant partnerships with local and national cultural institutions. She also developed a series of forums, such as *Creole Sweet: The Praline and Its World* and published *High on the Hog: A Culinary Journey from Africa to America* (2011).

On July 1, 2012, Dillard University inaugurated Dr. Walter M. Kimbrough, its seventh president, setting a new course of leadership with this former president of Philander Smith College, a private historically black college in Little Rock, Arkansas. Kimbrough, affectionately known as the "Hip Hop Prez," is a leading scholar on the history of Hip Hop and black fraternities and sororities. Dr. Kimbrough and his esteemed wife, Adria Nobles Kimbrough, an accomplished lawyer and pre-law adviser for the Center of Law and Public Interest at Dillard University, have hosted many diverse and distinguished guests to date.

On April 18, 2013, Dr. Kimbrough launched a lecture series at Dillard University called "Brain Food," inviting a diverse array of guests to Dillard's campus, including author and Georgetown University professor, Michael Eric Dyson; first African-American Chairman of the Republican National Committee, Michael Steele; author of *Our Black Year* and co-founder of the Empowerment Experiment, Maggie Anderson; hip hop female pioneer and founder of the Hip Hop Sister Foundation, MC Lyte; and American Ballet Theatre soloist and author, Misty Copeland.

Menu from March 2016
Brain Food lecture

Before these public lectures, Dr. Kimbrough and Mrs. Kimbrough invite select faculty, students, and community members to share an intimate dining experience with the honored guest lecturer. "Speakers can have more meaningful interaction with the students, and we have a responsibility to show that our education and experiences are just as good (as other institutions). These are people to whom these students may not have been exposed. It also gives faculty members an opportunity to tie in their curriculum to their presentations."[16] Dr. Kimbrough also invites incoming students to have lunch with him to welcome them to campus and to understand their needs. "I sometimes become a father to those who don't have one." Every Thanksgiving, the Kimbroughs open their home to students, faculty, and staff.

Dillard Campus, 2019

In 2014, Zella Palmer was appointed as the second chair of the Dillard University Ray Charles Program in African-American Material Culture. Palmer launched the Dr. Rudy Joseph Lombard lecture series at Dillard University in honor of the late culinary historian. Lombard had co-authored, along with Chef Nathaniel Burton, *Creole Feast: 15 Master Chefs of New Orleans Reveal Their Secrets* (1978), the only comprehensive

cookbook documenting the history and legacy of New Orleans black chefs. Under Palmer's leadership, the Ray Charles Program launched the program's inaugural conference on April 16, 2015, *The Story of New Orleans Creole Cooking: The Black Hand in the Pot*, with keynote speaker and culinary historic interpreter, Michael Twitty. In partnership with the Whitney Plantation, the Ray Charles Program hosted a cooking demo in their historic kitchen with Twitty. Other invitees included local scholars such as Whitney Plantation Academic Director, Dr. Ibrahima Seck, and New Orleans civil rights activist, A.P. Tureaud Jr.

Dillard University Ray Charles Program Chef Pierre Thiam

The inaugural conference celebrated the rich culinary history brought from the shores of West Africa, Central Africa, and the Caribbean by enslaved Africans and Haitian émigrés who were creolized in the Crescent City with enslaved Africans, farmers, cooks, street vendors, and *gens de couleur libre* (free people of color). In 2015, Palmer and select Ray Charles Program students began filming *The Story of New Orleans Creole Cooking: The Black Hand in the Pot* documentary. In 2018, Palmer and Dr. Caretta Cooke launched Life After Dillard: Dining Etiquette 101, a workshop that teaches students dining etiquette for any setting.

Dillard University Ray Charles Program, March 27, 2017

The Ray Charles Program in African-American Material Culture continues to invite guest lecturers, develop student curricula, and serve as a repository for African-American material culture in New Orleans and the South. Ray Charles and Dr. Rudy Joseph Lombard understood that "black Involvement in the New Orleans Creole cuisine is as old as gumbo and is just as important."[17]

Dillard University embraces the "town and gown" relationships by bringing together the university, community, and the larger public. The community cookbooks printed under the Dent and

Cook administrations are evident of this merger. Both community cookbooks embrace and lift up the glory of African-American material culture in New Orleans and the South. They epitomize their eras and solidify Dillard University as a mecca for critical thinking and a higher learning institution that preserves and celebrates New Orleans culture and cuisine.

This historic cookbook is divided into three sections. The first section re-prints recipes from the Albert W. Dent presidency and the *The Dillard Women's Club Cookbook: A Collection of Fine Recipes including Louisiana Cuisine, Foreign Dishes and Favorite Family Recipes*. The second section reprints recipes from the Samuel Dubois Cook presidency and the *The Dillard Auxiliary's International Food Festival Cookbook*. The final section, *Fair Dillard: A Collection of Contemporary Recipes,* includes recipes from Dr. Walter M. Kimbrough's presidency.

Mardi Gras Indian Queen Cherice Harrison Nelson and mother Hearest Harrison passing down recipes to the next generation

Each president left an indelible mark on the institution, its students, and the community. Their legacy of embracing the notables of the day, faculty, staff, students, and the local community into this rich gumbo stands high in the history of great historically black colleges and universities. Dillard University has a rich culinary history spanning 150 years of tradition, inviting students, faculty and staff, community, and prominent figures to engage and eat with the Dillard family. This cookbook chronicles the relationships built over decades and is dedicated to Dillard alumni and students who have fond memories of Fair Dillard.

The Dillard Women's Club Cookbook:
A Collection of Fine Recipes including Louisiana Cuisine, Foreign Dishes, and Favorite Family Recipes

The Dillard Women's Club Cookbook: *A Collection of Fine Recipes including Louisiana Cuisine, Foreign Dishes, and Favorite Family Recipes* (1958) comprises recipes gathered from friends and guests of the third president of Dillard University, Albert W. Dent and First Lady Mrs. Ernestine Jessie Covington Dent. Albert Dent was president of Dillard from 1941 to 1969. His tenure coincided with a period of rigid segregation in the South, when African-Americans were prohibited from public places, including concert halls, hotels, and restaurants. For this reason, African-Americans often entertained in their homes. But Dillard helped fill the void for public arts experiences, such as music and the performing arts, lectures by persons of national note, and other intellectual and cultural presentations for the students as well as the public; and these activities brought many guests to its campus.

Below: Page from Dent family guestbook with Duke Ellington, Jackie Robinson, and Jim Brown as guest entries

The Dents hosted nationally renowned visitors to the city of New Orleans and Dillard University in their beautiful home on Dillard's campus. First Lady of Dillard University for twenty-nine years, Mrs. Dent was a hostess *par* excellence, a gracious and warm woman who was admired by all who knew her and knew of her. She entertained with exquisite style, with elegant dinners and receptions for her guests and always flowers galore. A list of their guests who stayed in the president's home includes luminaries such as Eleanor Roosevelt, Ralph Bunche,

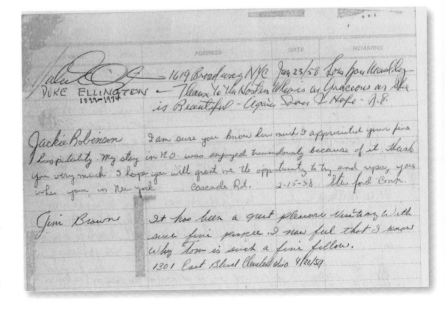

Emperor Haile Selassie, Paul Robeson, and a host of other dignitaries. Mrs. Dent was without peer in entertainment. As First Lady of Dillard, she was the epitome of grace and a role model for the students. Mrs. Dent was a dear friend of my mother and I have many fond memories of attending events at Dillard University and dinners at the Dents' home. At that time, there was a lot of faculty housing on campus. It was a welcoming place for all generations and students. Later in life, I attended Dillard University when they offered courses in education, and Dillard will always hold a special place in my heart.

Through the years, Mrs. Dent gathered the recipes of her friends, her many guests, visitors to Dillard, and members of organizations that she was affiliated with, including the Links, Inc., the Louisiana Philharmonic Symphony Orchestra, the New Orleans Garden Club, and others too numerous to mention. There was no one to compare to her during that time. The university allowed her to bring the who's who of African-Americans to Dillard and entertain them in grand style. Mrs. Dent was the first African-American to sit on New Orleans Symphony Orchestra's board.

Reverend Elliot Mason speaking at an alumni dinner hosted by the Dents.

President Dent (far left), wife Jessie Dent (far right), and their three sons

Although she was an accomplished musician and graduate of Juilliard, in those days a woman's career ended when she married.

I am sure that some of the dishes in this cookbook are the very ones she served her guests. This cookbook is without peer in the vast array of people who contributed and Mrs. Dent preserved the recipes lovingly.

I recognize many of the contributors to this cookbook, some of whom were friends of my mother. My mother, Mrs. C.C. Haydel, even contributed a Crayfish Bisque recipe that I still cherish to this day. Many recipes are family dishes handed down through the generations. I also shared three recipes in the "Fair Dillard" section, recipes that were passed down to me from my grandmother and mother, such as Creole Jambalaya, Grans Filè Gumbo, and my mother's Creole White Beans. This cookbook is a treasure trove from famous luminaries and ordinary people who visited Dillard University throughout the decades.

This is an extraordinary collection of recipes you will find nowhere else and is one of the many legacies of Mrs. Ernestine Jessie Covington Dent.

Dillard University letter from the
Women's Club detailing plans for a cookbook

Sybil Haydel Morial
Former First Lady of New Orleans

Note to reader: *The Dillard Women's Club Cookbook: A Collection of Fine Recipes including Louisiana Cuisine, Foreign Dishes and Favorite Family Recipes* was printed in 1958. We decided to reprint the original recipes as they were printed. Zella Palmer, the Chair of the Dillard University Ray Charles Program in African-American Material Culture, has contributed additional notes to the reader.

DILLARD
WOMEN'S
CLUB

COOK
BOOK

RECIPE FOR A GOOD LIFE
****

"Take equal parts of kindness, unselfishness and thoughtfulness; mix in an atmosphere of love; add the spice of usefulness; scatter a few grains of cheerfulness; season with smiles; stir in a hearty laugh, and

DISPENSE TO EVERYBODY."

Reprinted from The Pittsburg Courier

A Few Favorite RECIPES From A Few Favorite Friends

We proudly present the following extraordinary collection of select personal recipes, graciously contributed by Friends of Dillard University who have achieved world-wide acclaim and recognition, beginning with our most famous "First Lady of the World" Mrs. Franklin D. Roosevelt.

"On my arrival in New Orleans Dr. A. E. Dent, president of Dillard University, met me and we went directly to the university where I held a press conference. This was recorded for television and it was a rather novel experience for me. . . .

"The Dillard University campus is lovely, with broad lawns and simple white buildings that are all very harmonious. A row of trees runs down the center of the campus, which is patterned after Thomas Jefferson's plan at the University of Virginia. The U.N. flags were displayed back of the speaker's stand and the only ceremony was the playing of the 'Star-Spangled Banner' by some high school bands and some singing by the choir of the university...

"Dillard is one of the universities participating in the United Negro College Fund and I think it is doing a very good job choosing its faculty, which is interracial. The same is true of the student body, and the school is constantly striving to raise the standards of scholarship. I am sure this university offers as good an opportunity for sound education as one can find in the area.

"I enjoyed my parting lunch with some members of the faculty at Dr. Dent's house, and I made a three-thirty plane home."

–Mrs. Eleanor Roosevelt, April 2, 1953

HUCKLEBERRY DESSERT
Mrs. Eleanor Roosevelt

INGREDIENTS:
- 1 loaf of sliced (white) bread
- 2 ½ cups of huckleberries
- ¼ cup of sugar

DIRECTIONS:
Line the sides and bottoms of a glass casserole dish with slices of bread, not too fresh, from which crusts have been removed. Pour in some stewed huckleberries. Add another layer of bread; continue to alternate bread and berries until dish is filled. Place in refrigerator overnight. Serve plain or with whipped cream.

In the original recipe only the directions were given. There was no list of ingredients or measurements. I added a list of ingredients with measurements based on the recipe's cooking directions. I also added sugar as an ingredient. In a saucepan, combine the huckleberries, sugar, and ⅓ cup of water and bring to a boil. Lower the heat and cook uncovered over medium-low heat, stirring occasionally for 6 to 8 minutes. The huckleberries will be slightly cooked and the juice from the berries will become a syrup. Turn off the heat. Ladle the huckleberry mixture over the bread. Refrigerate overnight. Serve with whipped cream.

SOUTH AMERICAN PUDDING
Marian Anderson

INGREDIENTS:
- 1 ½ dozen ladyfingers
- ½ cup of butter
- ½ cup of sugar
- 2 egg yolks
- currant or cranberry or strawberry jam

DIRECTIONS:
Cream butter and sugar and egg yolks until light and fluffy. Sprinkle ladyfingers with wine, better yet, dip them with wine. Then line a tart pan with ladyfingers, a layer of butter cream, a layer of jam, and repeat the process until the materials have been used. Place the pan in the refrigerator for two or more hours. Before serving, spread the pudding with stiffly whipped cream. Serve on chilled plates.

The original recipe does not include wine in the list of ingredients. I suggest using a sweet Riesling wine and lightly dipping the ladyfingers in a bowl with the wine. It also does not include heating directions. I suggest preheating your oven to 375 degrees and baking the pudding for 8 minutes.

"Marian Anderson, world-famous contra-alto opera singer performed at the Lincoln Memorial in Washington, D.C., in 1939 and became the first African-American to perform at the Metropolitan Opera in New York City in 1955. Ernestine Jessie Covington Dent's, First Lady of Dillard University, love for music, entertaining, and inviting famous African Americans of the times to Dillard University included a friendship with Anderson. Dillard University music students volunteered as ushers for a segregated concert at New Orleans Municipal Auditorium in 1940 that hosted Anderson. Anderson was also invited to attend a dinner at the Longvue home of longtime supporters of Dillard University Edgar and Edith Stern. Edith Stern, daughter of Julius Rosenwald, a staunch supporter and philanthropist of education for African-Americans, invited Marian Anderson to dine at the Sterns home. An interracial dinner at one of the most prominent elite New Orleanian's home was unprecedented for the time."

–Edith Stern, *Autobiography of a House* manuscript (1970)

Dr. Mary McLeod Bethune, educator, pioneer, civil rights activist, founder of the National Council of Negro Women, and advisor to United States President Franklin D. Roosevelt delivered Dillard University's commencement address in 1951.

OLD FASHIONED BROWN SUGAR COOKIES
Dr. Mary McLeod Bethune

INGREDIENTS:

- 3 cups of flour
- 1 cup of brown sugar
- 1 cup of white sugar
- 1 cup of shortening
- 3 eggs
- 1 teaspoon of cooking baking soda
- 2 tablespoons of heavy cream
- 1 teaspoon of allspice
- 1 teaspoon of cinnamon (powder)
- 1 teaspoon of mace
- 1 teaspoon of nutmeg
- ½ teaspoon of ginger (powder)
- ½ teaspoon of cloves (powder)
- ½ cup of shredded coconut
- 1 teaspoon of vanilla extract
- 1 cup of chopped nuts
- ½ cup of candied orange peel

DIRECTIONS:

Mix all ingredients in a bowl. Drop by tablespoon on greased cookie sheet. Cook in moderate oven. Makes 4 dozen cookies.

 Preheat oven to 375 degrees. Roll rounded tablespoonfuls of the cookie dough into 1-inch balls and place on a greased cookie sheet. Bake 10–12 minutes. Remove to wire racks to cool completely.

CREAMED SWEETBREADS
Ralph J. Bunche

INGREDIENTS:

- 6 sweetbreads
- ½ cup of lemon juice
- ½ teaspoon of salt

FOR SAUCE:

- 3 tablespoons of butter
- 4 tablespoons of good sherry
- 3 tablespoons of flour
- ¾ cup of milk
- ¾ cup of heavy cream
- Salt to taste

DIRECTIONS:

Boil sweetbreads in water to which lemon juice and salt have been added. When cold, cut into ½ or ¾ inch cubes. To make sauce: melt butter in a saucepan, add flour, and cook slowly until bubbly but not brown. Add milk, cream, and salt, stirring constantly and cook until sauce is thickened. Add sherry, combine sauce with sweetbreads, and serve hot. Makes 4 to 5 servings.

Ralph J. Bunche, American diplomat, Howard University political science professor, civil rights activist, and Nobel Peace Prize, winner gave a speech at Dillard University for the Embree Memorial Lecture in the 1930s.

- -

JANSSON'S TEMPTATION (Swedish)
Mattiwilda Dobbs

INGREDIENTS:

- 4 white potatoes
- 1 tablespoon of butter
- 1 can of anchovy filets
- 1 sliced small yellow onion
- 1 cup of heavy cream

DIRECTIONS:

Cut 4 or 5 raw white potatoes into fine strips; place in buttered fire-proof casserole dish. Cover with anchovy filets, thinly sliced onion, and butter. Cover with cream and bake 1 hour in a 400 degree oven. Add more cream if dry. Serve hot as an hors d'oeurve or snack.

 In the original recipe only the directions were given. There was no list of ingredients or measurements. I added a list of ingredients with measurements based on the recipe's cooking directions.

Mattiwilda Dobbs, African-American opera singer for the Metropolitan Opera, was a friend of Ernestine Jessie Covington Dent.

Natalie Hinderas, pianist and composer, attended Oberlin Conservatory of Music with Ernestine Jessie Covington Dent.

LE NOUVEAU RICHE POULE (Part I)
Natalie Hinderas

INGREDIENTS:

- 1 whole chicken (deboned)
- 1 cup of chopped scallions
- 1 chopped stalk of celery
- 1 diced green bell pepper
- 1 cup of chopped parsley
- Salt and pepper
- 1 teaspoon of chopped garlic
- ½ cup of cooking sherry

DIRECTIONS:

Cut chicken into parts; brown in Crisco until golden brown. Add chopped scallions, celery, pepper, and parsley as desired. Season with salt, pepper, and garlic. Salt to taste. Cover with boiling water and add ½ cup of cooking sherry. Cook until tender. Remove from liquid and serve.

CHICKEN SALADE (Part II)

INGREDIENTS:

- 1 chicken (as prepared above) cut in bite-size pieces
- ¼ cup of diced olives
- 1 can of pimento
- ¼ cup of diced pickles
- 1 can of artichoke hearts
- 2 slices of cooked bacon
- ¼ cup of chopped almonds
- 2 cups of mayonnaise
- ¼ cup of sour cream
- Salt and pepper to taste
- 1 teaspoon of sugar
- A dash of nutmeg
- 1 head of lettuce

DIRECTIONS:

Mix all ingredients and toss with dressing made from mayonnaise, sour cream, and Buccaneer Dressing. (If this dressing is not available, add garlic salt). Add salt, pepper, sugar, and a dash of nutmeg. Serve on crisp lettuce and (optional) garnish with carrot curls, tomato quarters, black olives, and boiled eggs.

EAST INDIAN CHICKEN
Lena Horne

Part I:
INGREDIENTS:

- 4 pounds (whole) chicken
- 2 bay leaves
- 2 cloves
- ¼ pound of butter
- 1 cup of celery leaves
- 1 small onion, chopped
- 1 tablespoon of curry powder
- 2 quarts of water

DIRECTIONS:

Place chicken in pot with other ingredients, simmer until tender, cool, strain stock, and cut chicken from bone in large pieces.

Part II:
INGREDIENTS:

- ½ pound of butter
- 1 teaspoon of seasoned salt
- 1 bunch of chopped green onions
- 1 pint of half and half
- ½ cup of chopped celery
- ½ pint of heavy cream
- ½ cup of chopped parsley
- Remaining chicken stock
- 2 chopped green peppers
- 2 diced pimentos
- 2 tablespoons of paprika
- ½ cup of chopped salted almonds
- 2 tablespoons of curry powder
- 6–8 ripe olives, sliced
- ½ cup of flour
- ½ cup of chopped chutney
- 2 cups of pineapple juice
- 1 cup of rice
- 1 tablespoon of fresh grated coconut
- 1 handful of raisins

DIRECTIONS:

Sauté onions, celery, parsley, peppers in butter with paprika and curry. Add flour, blend, and add salt, milk, and cream plus stock from cooking chicken, chutney, and other ingredients. Simmer 30 minutes. Serve curry around a mound of pineapple rice. (Make this by cooking rice in pineapple juice). Garnish with fresh grated coconut and raisins.

Lena Horne was an actress, singer, and civil rights activist. Her producer Sherman Sneed was a Dillard University graduate and had played football there. Sneed was cast as Jim in Porgy and Bess, *co-produced the Broadway show,* Lena Horne: The Lady and Her Music, *and was a back up singer for Harry Belafonte.*

VIRGINIA GENTLEMAN STEAK DINNER

(A favorite of the late Charles S. Johnson)

Mrs. Charles S. Johnson

Dr. Charles S. Johnson, first African-American president of Fisk University, had a strong relationship with Dr. Will W. Alexander and Dr. Albert W. Dent. He was a candidate for Dillard University's Presidency. Mrs. Marie Antoinette Burgette-Johnson, wife of Dr. Charles S. Johnson, was the daughter of an African-American caterer in Wisconsin for wealthy white families. Mrs. Johnson was known for her graciousness and hospitality at Fisk University.

INGREDIENTS:

- 1 round steak
- 1 tablespoon of salt
- 1 cup of flour
- 2 sliced green peppers
- 2 chopped medium onions
- Salt and pepper to taste

DIRECTIONS:

Place round steak on cutting board, mix 1 level tablespoon of salt into 1 cup of flour and sprinkle over steak. Beat with a meat pounder, shake off extra flour and turn steak. Beat rest of flour into reverse side of the steak. Cut steak into individual portions about 4 x 5 inches. Place ¼ cup of shortening into iron skillet and heat. Sauté steak on both sides until brown. Put one quart of water into a Dutch oven and add 2 green peppers, sliced and 2 medium onions, chopped. Boil and then drop steak into boiling water. Pour excess fat from skillet, add 1 cup of water into skillet. Bring to a boil and add to meat and vegetables in the Dutch oven. Cover tightly and simmer for one hour.

 MENU

Broiled Grapefruit
Buttermilk Biscuits
Virginia Steak with Peppers
Cole Slaw
Mashed Potatoes
Sweet Potato Pie
Stewed Tomatoes

ITALIAN SPAGHETTI
Toki Schalk Johnson

INGREDIENTS:

- 3 onions, chopped
- 1 package of thin spaghetti
- 3 green peppers, chopped
- Parsley sprigs
- 1 bunch of celery, chopped
- Marjoram
- 2 pods garlic
- Thyme
- 2 large cans of tomatoes
- Red pepper flakes
- 1 ½ pounds of ground steak
- Celery seeds
- Salt and pepper
- Parmesan cheese, grated

DIRECTIONS:

Sauté onion, green pepper, celery, garlic, and parsley in a small amount of fat. When sufficiently cooked, medium brown, add ground meat and brown gently. In stew pan, mix tomatoes and tomato paste, add seasonings. Add meat and onion-pepper mixture and simmer for at least 3 hours, stirring occasionally to keep from sticking. The sauce will be thick with a trace of oil on top when cooked. Cook thin spaghetti to medium firmness, don't overcook, and serve plates placing sauce on top. Sprinkle parmesan cheese over all, and pass the pepper flakes for those who like it really hot.

Toki Schalk Johnson, celebrated journalist and society columnist for the African-American newspaper, The Pittsburgh Courier *and first African-American to be a member of the Women's Press Club gave a speech at Dillard University in 1947.*

Etta Moten, actress and singer, played Bessie in Porgy and Bess. *Moten was married to the founder of the Associate Negro Press, Claude Barnett. Moten gave a speech at Dillard University in the 1970s.*

INDONESIAN CHICKEN (African Groundnut Stew)
Etta Moten

INGREDIENTS:

- 1 ½ cups of uncooked rice
- ½ teaspoon of mace
- 4 cups of chicken broth
- ½ teaspoon of chili powder
- 1 ½ teaspoons of salt
- ¼ cup of peanut butter
- ¼ pound of butter
- 1 cup of cooked crabmeat
- 4 very large onions, chopped
- 1 cup of cubed baked ham
- 1 garlic clove, minced
- 1 cup of cooked chicken
- 1 teaspoon whole cumin seed
- 1 cup of chopped peanuts
- 1 pound of uncooked shrimp
- 1 cup of shredded browned coconut
- 3 (ripe) bananas, sliced

DIRECTIONS:

Put rice in saucepan. Add 3 cups of chicken broth and salt. Bring to a boil, then cover with a lid and simmer 15 minutes. Remove from heat and let stand 10 minutes. While rice cooks, sauté onions, garlic, and cumin in butter for 10 minutes. Add peeled de-veined shrimp to onions and cook for 10 minutes. Stir in coriander, mace, chili powder, peanut butter, and mix well. Add crab meat, ham, chicken, and remaining 1 cup of chicken broth. Heat until very hot. Gently stir rice into shrimp mixture. Serves 8. Good with Sauterne. Allow each guest to serve himself. Peanuts, coconut, and sliced bananas are placed on top of each serving.

STANDARD BLUEBERRY MUFFINS
Mrs. Charlotte Wallace Murray

INGREDIENTS:

- ½ cup of butter
- 2 cups of all-purpose flour
- 1 cup of sugar
- 4 teaspoons of baking powder
- 1 cup of milk
- ¼ teaspoon of salt
- 2 eggs
- ½ teaspoon of cinnamon
- ½ cup of blueberries

DIRECTIONS:

Cream butter and sugar; add milk and beaten eggs. Sift together dry ingredients and combine mixtures to make a batter. Have blueberries dry. Grease a muffin pan and fill each tin one-third full of batter and cover each with 1 teaspoon of berries. Add enough batter to fill each tin two-thirds full. Bake 25 minutes in a moderate oven. Makes 16 large muffins.

Charlotte Wallace Murray taught and studied music in the Washington, D.C. area from 1906-1915. After moving to New York City she continued her studies and performing. In 1926, she earned the role of "Queen" in the opera Deep River, *which featured the first mixed race opera cast in the United States.*

- -

PAIN PATATE (Creole Potato Pone)
Camille Lucie Nickerson

INGREDIENTS:

- 6 medium sized sweet potatoes
- ¾ cup of sugar
- ½ teaspoon of salt
- ¾ cup of milk
- 1 tablespoon of shortening
- Dash of black pepper

DIRECTIONS:

Grate sweet potatoes to make three cups. Mix potatoes, sugar, milk, salt, pepper, and melted shortening. Blend and stir well. Grease a bowl or deep pan. Pour in mixture; bake in a moderate oven for 90 minutes.

Camile Lucie Nickerson, a New Orleans native, was a graduate of Oberlin College, singer for the National Negro Opera Company, and music professor at Howard University. Nickerson composed and published Creole music. Nickerson's family were well known musicians in New Orleans and her father established the music program at Straight University.

CRAB MEAT a la CAPAHOSIC
Fred D. Patterson

INGREDIENTS:

- 3 cups of crabmeat
- 1 cup of chopped green pepper
- 5 eggs, well beaten
- 1 cup of chopped onions
- 2 tablespoons of butter
- 1 cup of chopped celery
- Salt, pepper
- Worcestershire sauce
- Tabasco sauce to taste

DIRECTIONS:

Mix celery, pepper, and onions together. Place in a wide bottomed pan and barely cover with water. Boil until tender and water has evaporated. Mix beaten eggs and crabmeat; add seasonings to taste. Add butter to vegetable mixture, then add crabmeat mixture. Blend well and cook slowly until of the desired consistency. Serve on a platter. Garnish with parsley and crisp bacon strips.

Fred D. Patterson, founder of the United Negro College Fund and former president of Tuskegee University, maintained a strong relationship with Dr. Albert W. Dent. Patterson gave a speech at Dillard University in 1958.

- -

BACON EGGS AND MUSHROOMS
"a la desperación"
Ira de Augustine Reid

INGREDIENTS:

- 4 eggs
- ½ pound of melted butter
- 1 can of mushrooms
- Fresh chopped parsley and chives

DIRECTIONS:

Break 4 eggs carefully into a buttered baking dish. Add ½ cup of canned mushroom pieces. Season to taste. Add ¼ pound of melted butter. Bake in a slow oven, 325 degrees for about 20 minutes. Garnish with chopped parsley and chives. Serve from baking dish with cooked bacon.

Ira de Augustine Reid, sociologist, author, and professor, was a graduate of Morehouse College. Reid published nine books on the social conditions of African-Americans in the 1930s.

AUTUMN JOY
Philippa Duke Schuyler

INGREDIENTS:

- 2 pounds of raisins, ground fine
- 1 lemon peel, ground with raisins
- 1 teaspoon of ground cloves
- 1 stick of sweet butter (softened by room heat)
- 2 pounds of apples
- Whipped cream

DIRECTIONS:

Mix raisins and lemon peel, cloves and butter together. Peel, slice, and chop apples. Add to raisins mixture. Serve with whipped cream.

Philipa Duke Schuyler, a famous child prodigy and pianist throughout the 1930s and 1940s, performed twice at Dillard University. Schuyler was also a pioneer in the vegan lifestyle. Mrs. Dent threw a party for her.

EGGS BENEDICT
William J. Trent Jr.

INGREDIENTS:

- 4 English muffins
- 1 ½ cups of Hollandaise sauce
- 4 slices of ham
- ½ cup of truffles
- 4 eggs

DIRECTIONS:

Gently pull apart muffins (do not cut them). Brown muffins slightly under the broiler and butter generously. Cut ham to approximately the size of the muffins and broil. Poach eggs. Place a slice of ham on each muffin and then place a poached egg on each slice of ham. Ladle Hollandaise sauce generously over eggs and top with truffles.

William J. Trent Jr. was the former Executive Director of the United Negro College Fund. Trent maintained a strong relationship with Dr. Albert W. Dent. Trent gave a speech at Dillard University in 1958.

Howard Thurman was a theologian, author, philosopher, graduate of Morehouse College, and the first African-American faculty appointed to Boston University. Thurman authored twenty books including his most famous work Jesus and the Disinherited *(1949). Thurman delivered the dedication sermon for Dillard University's Chapel. His wife, Sue Bailey Thurman, was an accomplished author, civil rights activist, and historian. Sue Bailey was a graduate of Spelman College and founder of the* Aframerican Women's Journal.

THE THURMAN'S ANNUAL "12th NIGHT WASSAIL"

Howard and Sue Bailey Thurman

INGREDIENTS:

- 1 gallon of apple cider
- 2 (4-inch) sticks of cinnamon
- 1 quart of orange juice
- 4 tablespoons of whole cloves
- 1 quart of pineapple juice
- 4 tablespoons of whole allspice
- 1 cup of lemon juice
- 1 teaspoon of mace
- 1 cup of lime juice
- 1 teaspoon of freshly ground nutmeg
- 1 pint of sugar (or to taste)
- 1 quart of canned spiced crabapples

DIRECTIONS:

Mix all fruit juices and spices together, heat slowly and simmer for 15 minutes, being careful never to bring to a boil. Add bright red canned spiced crabapples and continue heating 5 minutes longer. Put an apple for each serving in individual punch cups or silver bowl. Drink as you assemble around the fire to watch the glowing embers from the "burning of the holiday green."

"We have served some variant of this recipe on each occasion since the Twelfth Night celebration was established in our home twenty-five years ago. Traditionally there must be the balance in taste of five fruits and five spices. However, the real 'magic' for success in the formula comes at the moment when the hostess stirs into the mixture deep thoughts and wishes for the happiness and well-being of the community of friends with whom we are all united, in every crack and cranny of our world."

SPINACH BALLS
Mrs. Robert L. Vann

DIRECTIONS:

Prepare mashed potatoes as though they were to be served for a meal. Cook, drain, and season spinach with butter, salt, and pepper. Take a small portion of spinach and cover with potatoes while still hot. Place in refrigerator for several hours or until firm. Dip in egg and cracker crumbs and fry in deep fat. They should be about the size of a small orange. The amount used depends on the number of people to be served.

Robert L. Vann was the publisher of the African American newspaper The Pittsburgh Courier *from 1912 until his death in 1940.*

CHAMPIGNONS au VIN (Mushrooms in Wine)
Leontyne Price and William Warfield

INGREDIENTS:

- 1 cup of small fresh mushrooms
- 2 teaspoons of sugar
- 1 tablespoon of butter
- 1 teaspoon of vinegar
- 1 tablespoon of sauterne
- 1 celery stalk, chopped
- Salt and cayenne pepper to taste
- 1 tablespoon of lemon juice

DIRECTIONS:

Peel and wash mushrooms; sauté lightly in butter. Remove mushrooms from fire. Make a sauce by mixing the remaining ingredients. Add sauce to mushrooms and simmer 2 or 3 minutes. Cool and place in refrigerator. Serve cold.

Leontyne Price, famous opera singer and graduate of Central State University, performed at many concerts for the Metropolitan Opera and around the globe. Pryce married William Warfield, a noted baritone singer in 1952. The Dents brought the famed couple to Dillard University to perform at Dillard University's Chapel dedication in 1955.

POTATO SPLITS
Mrs. J. Ernest Wilkins

DIRECTIONS:

Mix 1 cup of flour with 1 teaspoon of salt and 2 tablespoons of sugar in a mixing bowl. Scald 1 cup of milk, put in it (add) a ¾ cup of shortening and 1 cup of mashed potatoes. When lukewarm, pour into flour mixture. Put in 2 unbeaten eggs and beat lightly but mix thoroughly. Dissolve 1 package of yeast in about ⅓ cup of warm water. Pour into above mixture. Stir. Use about 3 cups more of flour or just enough to make a light dough when put into above mixture. Cover and let stand in a warm place for 2 hours or until double in bulk. Make into Parkerhouse rolls or clover leaf rolls, brush with butter and let stand 2 hours. Bake 15 or 20 minutes in a 400 degree oven. Makes 4 dozen rolls.

J. Ernest Wilkins was a lawyer and former Undersecretary of Labor for International Labor Affairs for United States President Dwight D. Eisenhower. His wife, Lucille Robinson, was a lawyer and former Board of Trustee for Dillard University.

Fannie C. Williams, adored New Orleans educator, was a graduate of Straight College. Williams was the former principal of New Orleans Valena C. Jones School and member of Dillard University Board of Trustees.

PLAIN MUFFINS (My Favorite Recipe)
Miss Fannie C. Williams

INGREDIENTS:

- 1 egg
- 1 tablespoon melted shortening
- 1 cup of milk
- 1 teaspoon of salt
- 3 cups of flour
- 1 tablespoon of sugar
- 2 teaspoons of baking powder

DIRECTIONS:

Mix liquid ingredients together. Sift the flour, baking powder, salt, and sugar. Stir into liquid and beat well. Grease muffin tins well. Drop mixture with a spoon. Place in a oven preheated at 400 degrees and bake 20 minutes. Serve hot with melted butter and fig preserves. This recipe may be varied by adding ½ cup of blueberries, cranberries, whole kernel corn, raisins, or chopped peanuts.

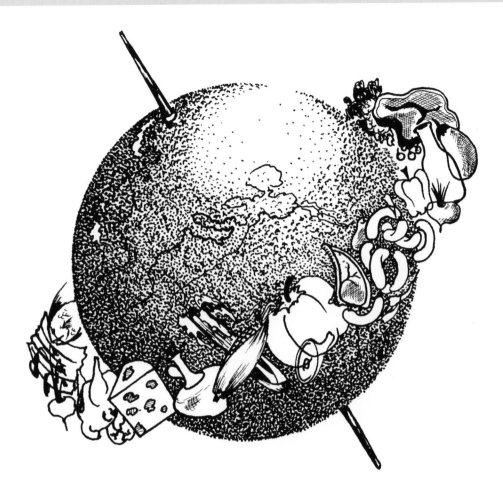

AROUND THE WORLD RECIPES

What's cooking—in other parts of the world? It is to be hoped that the following recipes of foreign cookery will serve to relieve the monotony of dishes to which we have become over-accustomed, and that they will provide interest and variety for static menus. We hope you will enjoy trying out these delightful recipes. They are offerings of personal friends who recommend them as their favorites among the exotic and delicious dishes of far-away lands.

CANTON PORK WITH PINEAPPLE SAUCE

Dr. Sauk Wong

Chinese

INGREDIENTS:

- 2 pounds of pork (tenderloin)
- ¼ teaspoon of fresh root ginger
  or powdered ginger
- 1 tablespoon of sugar
- ½ teaspoon of baking soda
- 1 teaspoon of brandy
  or 1 tablespoon of white wine
- 2 tablespoons of soy sauce
- 4 tablespoons of flour

DIRECTIONS:

Cut pork into ¾-inch cubes. Combine ginger, soy sauce, sugar, and spirits. Add to pork and let stand for 30 minutes. Mix flour and baking soda; add to pork and fry in deep fat.

ALMOND COFFEE TORTE

Mrs. Wilma Iggers

Czechoslovakian

INGREDIENTS:

Layers:
- 1 cup of sugar
- ¼ cup of almonds, scalded,
  peeled, and ground
- 6 egg whites
- ½ cup of flour

Filling:
- ¾ cup of sugar
- 4 well beaten egg yolks
- 1 tablespoon instant coffee
- ¾ cup of butter
- ½ cup of water, hot

DIRECTIONS:

Stir 1 cup of sugar with 3 of the egg whites until foamy. Add almonds. Beat other 3 egg whites with ¼ cup of sugar. Fold into almond mixture. Add ½ cup of flour. Bake in 3 thin layers in greased and floured cake pans for 15–20 minutes, 350 degree oven.

For Filling: Blend sugar, butter, egg yolks. Mix coffee with hot water, add a drop at a time. Cover layers, top, and sides of torte.

CHRISTMAS PUDDING

Mrs. Linda Furey

INGREDIENTS:

- 8 ounces of flour
- 3 ounces of grated raw carrots
- 1 teaspoon of baking powder
- 4 ounces of chopped raisins
- 4 ounces of Sultanas (or raisins)
- 1 heaping teaspoon of ground cinnamon
- 1 heaping tablespoon of mixed spice
- 3 eggs, fresh or dried
- 6 ounces of shredded suet
- 4 ounces of breadcrumbs
- 3 ounces of chopped apples
- About a gill of cider
    (Gill = 4 ounces)

DIRECTIONS:

Sift the flour and baking powder into a bowl and mix in the suet and breadcrumbs, then add the sifted sugar and spices. Add the dried fruit, grated carrots, chopped apples, and treacle and mix well. Beat the eggs and add, finally adding enough cider to make a stiffish mixture. Stir till the ingredients are well blended, then turn into one large or two smaller greased basins, cover with greased paper and a pudding cloth and steam for at least four hours. Remove the cloth and greased paper and when cool cover with a dry pudding cloth. Steam for at least 2 hours before serving. Serve with hard brandy sauce.

• •

YORKSHIRE PUDDING

Mrs. Linda Furey

INGREDIENTS:

- 1 pint of milk
- Pinch of fine salt
- 2 eggs
- Drippings
- 4 heaping tablespoons of flour

DIRECTIONS:

Put the flour and a good pinch of salt into a basin. Mix well. In the center, break in the eggs, stir gradually, mixing in with the flour from the sides, and add milk by degrees until a thick smooth batter is formed. Beat well for about 10 minutes, then add the remainder of milk, cover and let stand for at least 1 hour. When ready to use, cover the bottom of a pudding tin with a thin layer of drippings taken from the meat tin, and while the tin and drippings are getting thoroughly hot in the oven, give the batter another good beating. Bake for about 10 minutes in a hot oven. Serves 5 or 6. Serve with roast beef.

CHICKEN FRIED RICE

Yvonne Mason Burbridge

Indonesian

INGREDIENTS:

- ½ small onion, finely sliced
- 1 cup of cooked chicken
- ½ teaspoon of cayenne red pepper powder
- 2 tablespoons of oil or margarine
- Salt to taste
- 5 cups of fluffy boiled rice
- Soy sauce to taste

DIRECTIONS:

Fry onions and chicken in oil or margarine until light brown. Add cayenne pepper, salt, and stir. Add rice and stir well and constantly until rice looks a bit dry. Add soy sauce and stir again until rice has an even light brown color. This serves 4 people.

. . . .

CHATAZILIM – EGGPLANT AUBERGINE

The Israeli Embassy

Israeli

INGREDIENTS:

- 1 eggplant, large enough to make about 1 cup of pulp
- Juice of ½ lemon
- 2 tablespoons of mayonnaise or olive oil
- ½ onion, finely chopped
- Salt and pepper to taste

DIRECTIONS:

Place eggplant above an open flame and let it actually burn on all sides until soft. Cool and peel. Mash pulp with a fork until it is like a paste. Add onion, salt, pepper, and lemon juice. Stir in mayonnaise or olive oil or 1 tablespoon of each. Mix well. Serve on lettuce leaf as an appetizer. Garnish with slices of tomato and unpeeled cucumbers. Serves 6–8.

BIRD NEST PIE

Henrine Ward Banks

Italian

INGREDIENTS:

- 6 green peppers
- 3 teaspoons of olive oil
- 1 pound of ground beef
- Salt, pepper, cayenne pepper
- Garlic salt
- 6 tart apples
- 2 hard boiled eggs, sliced

DIRECTIONS:

Cut tops from peppers, remove core and seeds. Place in refrigerator. Mix ground beef, salt, pepper, garlic salt, and cayenne pepper. Cook in olive oil until brown. Cut tops from apples. Save. Peel and dice apples. Place peppers in a greased baking pan. Fill with alternate layers of apples, ground meat, and egg slices. Top stuffed peppers with apple tops. Sprinkle with garlic salt and butter. Bake in 230 degree oven for 15 to 20 minutes. Serve hot. Spaghetti and cheese may substitute for apple and egg.

BARONESS PUDDING

Florence Fraser

Jamaican

INGREDIENTS:

- ½ pound butter
- ½ pound brown sugar
- 4 eggs
- ½ pound bread
- ½ pound raisins
- ½ pound currants
- ¼ pound citron or peel
- ½ pound prunes, stewed
- ¼ pound nuts
- 1 glass of rum

DIRECTIONS:

Rub butter with brown sugar. Beat 4 eggs and add butter and sugar. Grate bread to crumbs and add remaining ingredients. Mix all together and add 1 wine glass of rum. Put into pudding mould and steam 2 hours. Serve with hard sauce.

CHAWAN MUSH (Steamed Chicken Custard)

Mrs. Galen Russell

Japanese

INGREDIENTS:

- 1 pint of chicken or fish soup (stock)
- ½ cup of cooked green vegetables, i.e. pea pods, beans, spinach
  In addition mushrooms and chestnuts may be added, or bamboo shoots
- 1 cup of chopped chicken and/or fish
- 1 teaspoon of salt
- 1 tablespoon of soy sauce
- 1 tablespoon of sugar
- 4–5 eggs

DIRECTIONS:

Mix thoroughly, then measure quantity, adding 2 well beaten eggs to each pint of the mixture. Cook in custard cups with lids on top by setting cups in water in oven or on top of stove until mixture sets like cup custard. Serve while hot in covered cups.

• •

SUKIYAKI

Mrs. Charles S. Johnson, Suggested by Dr. Jitsuichi Masuoka

Japanese

INGREDIENTS:

- 2 pounds of lean pork
- 1 cup of diced turnips
- 2 pounds of veal steak
- 1 pound of French style green beans
- 2 cups of chopped celery
- 1 can of water chestnuts
- 2 cups of diced onions
- 1 cup of soy sauce
- 3 green peppers, sliced
- ¼ cup of Chinese molasses
- 3 cups of diced cabbage
- 1 can of bean sprouts
- 1 tablespoon of salt

DIRECTIONS:

Place large roasting pan over burners, turn medium height. Cut meat into 1 x 2 inch chunks. Place pork in roaster stirring slowly until bottom of pan is lubricated. Then add veal, stirring until juices begin to flow. Add salt and molasses and stir. Add green beans, onions, celery, cabbage, and turnips stirring carefully after each addition so that vegetables remain firm. Add drained bean sprouts and water chestnuts gradually. Heat juices from sprouts and water chestnuts with ¼ cup of soy sauce. Add a ½ cup of juice to vegetables (save remainder for the table). Place on the pan with an air-tight cover. Remove from fire and allow to blend. Serve with rice. Serves 12.

JOLLOF RICE
Mrs. Prince A. Taylor

Liberian

INGREDIENTS:

- 1 cup of water
- 1 pound of beef, cut into small pieces
- 1 pound of fresh pork, cut in small pieces
- 1 cup of chicken, diced, optional small pieces
- 1 chopped onion
- 1 green pepper, chopped
- Bit of fresh hot pepper, chopped
- 2 tablespoons of fat
- Salt to taste
- 2 tablespoons of flour
- 1 cup of palm oil (or 1 stick of butter)
- 1 cup of tomatoes, sieved (or 1 cup of tomato paste)

DIRECTIONS:

Dredge meat and onion in the flour and brown in 2 tablespoons of fat. Add chopped peppers and simmer until tender, adding water if needed. When meat is tender and most of the water has evaporated, add chicken, tomatoes, and palm oil. Simmer for 5 minutes. Serve over hot rice.

 All chicken may be substituted for the meat. In this case, leave bones in chicken.

LIBERIAN PERLIEU RICE
Mrs. Louise Yancy, Monrovia, Liberia

Liberian

INGREDIENTS:

- 1 stewing chicken (2–3 pounds)
- 1 medium sized can of green peas
- 1 cup of salted pork or bacon, cubed
- 2 tablespoons of Crisco
- 1 cup of ham, chopped
- ½ can of tomato paste
- 3 cups of rice, uncooked
- 1 large onion, chopped
- 1 large green pepper, diced
- Salt to taste
- ½ teaspoon of black pepper
- 5 cups of water

DIRECTIONS:

Cut up chicken and season with salt, black pepper, and onion. Put fat in the pot, add chicken and bacon and fry for 5 minutes. Add water and rice; cook for 25 minutes. Add green pepper, ham, tomato paste, and let simmer. If necessary, add more water. Before moisture is completely absorbed, stir in green peas. Cover and let steam until grains of rice are well done. Serve hot. Garnish with a sliced hard boiled egg and a fresh chopped tomato.

CHICKEN CURRY WITH RICE
Mildred Hastings Swerdlow

Malayan

INGREDIENTS:

- 4 pounds of chicken, cut up
- ¼ cup of curry powder
- ½ teaspoon of powdered ginger
- 1 tablespoon of flour
- 1 cup of chicken broth
- ½ cup of diced onions
- 1 cup of sliced mushrooms
- ½ cup of diced celery
- Salt and pepper to taste
- Oil
- Golden rice

DIRECTIONS:

Sauté onion, garlic, and celery in oil until tender. In separate skillet, brown the cut up chicken in more oil, add sautéed vegetables, and cook slowly for about 1 hour, or until tender. Place broth in saucepan with mushrooms, curry powder, ginger, and flour. Heat gently, add mixture to chicken. When ready to serve, sprinkle soaked currants and grated coconut over top for a true Malayan touch. Serve with golden rice, passed separately. Serves 4–6.

Golden Rice:

To 3 cups of steamed white rice, add 1 teaspoon of powdered turmeric, diluted with a little chicken broth; add 2 tablespoons of melted butter; stir rice until lightly browned in a heavy skillet. Taste for seasoning. Minced chives, parsley, or shredded green onion tops may be added. Pine nuts, chopped cashews or pistachios, or slivered, blanched almonds give a fine flavor to golden rice. Pineapple bits sautéed in butter also give that extra something to the rice.

• •

ENCHILADAS
Mrs. Margaret Simms

Mexican

INGREDIENTS:

- 6 tortillas (cans are now available)
- 1 cup of canned tomatoes
- 1 cup of shredded lettuce
- 2 cloves of garlic, minced
- ½ cup of sharp cheese, grated
- 2 tablespoons of Wesson oil
- ½ pound of lean beef, ground or chopped in small cubes
- Season-All
- 1 medium onion (chopped)
- 1 cup of tomato paste

DIRECTIONS:

Sauté ½ pound of lean beef, ground or cubed, in Wesson oil, 1 medium sized onion and 2 cloves of garlic. When well browned, add 1 cup of tomato paste, 1 cup of canned tomatoes, 2 tablespoons of chili powder, salt, and Season-All powder. Let this simmer slowly until a deep red color is obtained. Place cooked ground meat between tortillas then add shredded lettuce, chopped onion, and grated cheese. Fold and fasten with toothpicks, pour sauce over the folded enchiladas and sprinkle with grated cheese. Heat in oven. Serve hot.

BEEF STROGANOFF

Mrs. Samuel C. Kincheloe

Russian

INGREDIENTS:

- 2 onions, cut very thin
- 6-ounce can of mushrooms
- ¼ cup of fat (butter, oleo, or other)
- Dash of Worcestershire sauce
- 2 ½ pounds of round steak cut in diagonal thin strips
- ½ pint of sour cream
- Salt and pepper to taste
- 1 can of tomato soup
- 1 tablespoon of prepared mustard

DIRECTIONS:

Sauté onions in fat (frying pan or Dutch oven). Add steak and brown. Pour in all other ingredients. Cover and cook slowly for an hour. Serves 5–7 people.

- -

CHICKEN BREASTS "VILLAROY"

Mattiwilda Dobbs

Spanish

DIRECTIONS:

Boil chicken breasts in water which has been seasoned with celery, onions, salt, pepper, garlic, and 2 cups of white wine. Cook until tender. Remove skin and bones without tearing flesh. Chill. Make a thick white sauce. Chill. Salt and pepper breasts; dip in cream sauce; dip in breadcrumbs; fry in deep fat. Serve with tomato sauce.

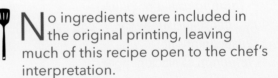

No ingredients were included in the original printing, leaving much of this recipe open to the chef's interpretation.

TURKISH DELIGHT
Phillipa Duke Schuyler

Turkish

INGREDIENTS:

- 2 pounds of seeded dates
- 1 stick of sweet butter
- 2 cups of whole powdered milk
- 1 teaspoon of nutmeg
- 1 cup of fresh almonds

DIRECTIONS:

Grind up dates. Mix dates with butter that is soft (but not heated); add nutmeg. Blend all of these with powdered milk until smooth. Shape with palms into long rolls. Chop almonds and turn the confection around the chopped (but not ground up) nuts so that the nuts cover the exterior. Place in icebox to stiffen overnight. Cut up in small pieces. Serve with fruit drinks.

• •

EASY HAMBURGERS OR MEAT LOAF
Louise Prothro

American

INGREDIENTS:

- 1 pound of ground beef (ground round or chuck)
- 1 cup of breadcrumbs (or ⅓ cup oatmeal)
- 1 teaspoon of salt
- ½ teaspoon of black pepper
- ¼ cup of grated onion
- ⅔ cup of evaporated milk (Pet)

DIRECTIONS:

Mix together gently with a fork or spoon. Shape into meat patties (8) or pat into loaf pan. Bake at 325 degrees.

CREOLE RECIPES

Creole cuisine was born of a blending of Louisiana seafoods and vegetables with ideas borrowed from excellent cooks from France, Spain, and Africa. Each hostess adds her own personal cooking skills, most of which can be summed up thus: the extraordinary use of seasonings and spices, plus the patience which only love for cooking can create. In these time tested recipes you will find romance of long-gone days.

CALAS (Rice Cakes)
Mildred Hastings Swerdlow

INGREDIENTS:

- ½ cup of rice
- 3 cups of water
- 3 eggs
- ½ cup of sugar
- ½ cake compressed yeast
- ½ teaspoon of grated nutmeg
- 3 tablespoons of flour
- Wesson oil or any mild cooking lard
- Powdered white sugar

DIRECTIONS:

Into 3 cups of boiling water put the rice, which has been thoroughly washed. Let it boil until it is very soft and mushy. Drain and set aside to cool. Dissolve yeast in ½ cup of hot water. When cold, mash well and mix rice with the yeast. Set the rice to rise overnight. In the morning, beat 3 eggs thoroughly, and add to the rice, mixing and beating well. Add a ½ cup of sugar and 3 tablespoons of flour to make the rice adhere. Mix well and beat thoroughly, bringing it to a thick batter. Set to rise for 15 minutes longer. Then add about a ½ teaspoonful of grated nutmeg and mix well. Heat oil in deep vessel, test by dropping a small cube of bread into it. If the bread becomes a golden brown the oil is ready. Drop the mixture from a large deep spoon, be sure that the cake does not touch the bottom of the pan. Fry to a golden brown. Sprinkle with the white powdered sugar, serve hot.

· ·

COURTBOUILLON a la CREOLE
Mrs. Edward E. Moore
Baton Rouge

INGREDIENTS:

- 3 pounds of sliced redfish or snapper
- 1 tablespoon of lard
- 12 well-mashed allspice or 1 rounded teaspoon
- 2 tablespoons of flour
- 3 sprigs of thyme
- 3 sprigs of sweet marjoram
- 3 sprigs of (fresh) parsley
- 1 large onion
- 1 clove of garlic
- 6 large fresh tomatoes
- 1 quart of water
- 1 lemon, juice
- 1 glass of claret
- Salt and cayenne to taste

DIRECTIONS:

Wash and clean fish thoroughly. Slice in fine pieces. Make a roux by heating 1 tablespoon of lard in a deep kettle. Add gradually 2 tablespoons of flour, stirring constantly. Add spices, garlic, and onion chopped very fine. Add 6 tomatoes chopped fine, or ½ can tomatoes. Pour in one glass of good claret, add 1 quart of water, and let it boil well. Then add salt and cayenne to taste. Boil for 5 minutes, then add fish, slice by slice. Add juice of 1 lemon and simmer for 10 minutes longer.

CRAB CUTLETS
Mrs. Julia Duncan

INGREDIENTS:

- 2 cups of crab meat
- 3 tablespoons of chopped onion
- 1 ¾ cups of cracker meal
- 2 tablespoons of chopped (fresh) parsley
- 2 eggs
- 1 green pepper, chopped
- ½ cup of milk
- 2 cloves of garlic, minced
- 1 teaspoon of salt
- Dash of cayenne pepper

DIRECTIONS:

Chop crabmeat, add seasonings, and mix well. Add whole eggs, milk, and 1 cup of cracker meal. Mold into croquettes, insert crab claw. Roll croquettes in the remaining cracker meal. Allow to chill in refrigerator for at least 1 hour. Just before serving, fry in a deep fat until golden brown. Serve with Julia's Red Sauce.

Julia's Red Sauce:

INGREDIENTS:

- 1 cup of hot milk
- 2 tablespoons of flour
- ½ cup of finely chopped pimento
- 1 teaspoon of paprika
- 1 tablespoon of lemon juice
- 2 tablespoons of sherry
- 2 egg yolks
- 3 tablespoons of butter
- Salt, pepper, and Tabasco sauce to taste

DIRECTIONS:

Melt butter in saucepan, add flour, blend, and slowly pour in milk, stirring constantly. Add pimento. Cook in double boiler for 10 minutes. When ready to serve, add well beaten egg yolks, lemon juice, seasonings, and sherry. Cook for 3 minutes. Serve on crab cutlets.

CRAB a la CASSEROLE
Mrs. Lydia G. Sindos

INGREDIENTS:

- 2 cups of crabmeat
- Celery salt (sparingly)
- Salt to taste
- Small piece of bay leaf
- Small piece of thyme
- 1 tablespoon of (fresh) chopped parsley
- 1 small hot green pepper, minced

DIRECTIONS:

Fold in 2 cups of crabmeat. If too thick, thin by adding Pet milk. Pour into buttered casserole, sprinkle and top with breadcrumbs, dot with butter. Bake in moderately hot oven about 25 minutes. Serve with hot buttered rolls, green tossed salad, or potato salad.

• •

DEVILED CRABS
Mrs. Bona V. Arnaud

INGREDIENTS:

- 1 pound of freshly picked crabs or frozen crab meat
- 1 tablespoon of mayonnaise
- 2 teaspoons of Worcestershire sauce
- 2 tablespoons of chopped green onion
- 2 tablespoons of McCormick Seafood seasoning
- 2 tablespoons of chopped parsley (fresh)
- ¼ cup of butter breadcrumbs
- 3 slices of stale bread

DIRECTIONS:

Melt butter in saucepan. Add onion, cook slowly; add crab meat with the mayonnaise, Worcestershire sauce, seafood seasoning, and parsley. Stir. Add the bread after soaking in a small amount of water if fresh crabs are used, in milk if frozen crabmeat is used. Place in aluminum foil crab shells. Top with bread-crumbs, dot with butter. Bake 30 minutes at 375 degrees.

CRAYFISH BISQUE
Mrs. Anita Gilbert

INGREDIENTS:

- 6 pounds crayfish
- ¼ cup of chopped onion
- ½ cup of chopped shallots
- 2 heaping tablespoons of flour
- ¼ cup of chopped (fresh) parsley
- 2 sprigs of (fresh) thyme
- ½ cup of chopped celery
- 2 bay leaves
- ¼ cup of butter or margarine
- ¾ cup of breadcrumbs
- ¼ teaspoon of ground thyme
- 1 beaten egg
- Salt, pepper, cayenne to taste

DIRECTIONS:

Sauce for bisque: Soak crayfish in salt water for 1 hour. Wash thoroughly. Scald and drain crayfish and set aside 24 heads. Place remaining heads in a large pot with 2 quarts of water. Add ½ of each kind of seasoning. Cook for 30 minutes; strain; add flour, 1 tablespoon of parsley, and simmer for one half hour. Sauté remaining seasonings in butter until lightly brown; add breadcrumbs and ¼ cup of broth. Remove from heat and add beaten egg. Stuff into crayfish heads; brown heads in a 400 degree oven. Add stuffed heads to sauce. Serve hot with rice if desired. Serves 6.

. . . .

CRAYFISH BISQUE
Mrs. C. C. Haydel

INGREDIENTS:

- 8 pounds of crayfish
- 1 large onion, chopped
- 1 bell pepper, chopped
- 4 pieces of celery, chopped
- 1 egg
- Salt, black and cayenne pepper to taste

DIRECTIONS:

Wash crayfish thoroughly and drop in unseasoned boiling water for 1 minute or until water again comes to boil. Drain, cool, and peel. Separate heads from tails. Remove yellow and white fat from heads to be used in gravy. Peel and chop tails with seasoning. Stuff heads and fry in deep fat until brown.

For Gravy: Same amount of seasoning except egg. Brown 1 tablespoon of flour, fry seasoning until well done. Add water, when gravy comes to a boil, add fat. Put heads in gravy and cook for 5 to 7 minutes.

FISH A LA HARRIET
Mrs. Harriett Holmes

INGREDIENTS:

- 1 fish (5 pounds)
- 1 teaspoon of vinegar
- 1 lemon
- Salt and pepper to taste
- 1 can of shrimp soup (stock)
- 1 can of mushroom soup (stock)

DIRECTIONS:

Boil fish in cheesecloth with seasoning about 30 minutes or until tender. Remove from water, cool. Remove scales and bones, place on platter. Blend together 1 can of shrimp soup and 1 can of mushroom soup with fish stock. Season to taste with salt, pepper, and Perrin sauce. Pour over fish, garnish with parsley and lemon slices.

· ·

FISH FILET CASSEROLE (With Cream Sauce)
Mrs. Lena Forcia Landry

INGREDIENTS:

- 1 tenderloined trout (2–3 pounds)
- 1 ½ dozen oysters
- Salt
- Pepper

Cream Sauce:

- ½ stick of butter
- Salt
- 1 tablespoon of flour
- Pepper
- 2 cups of liquid (oyster water and milk)
- ½ cup of chopped mushrooms

DIRECTIONS:

Cut slices of fish in half; season with salt and pepper. Roll four oysters in each piece of fish and secure with toothpicks. Place in a baking dish and close together. Pour cream sauce over the fish. Sprinkle cracker crumbs over the fish and bake in a moderate 350 degree oven for 40 minutes.

For Cream Sauce: Place liquid in a double boiler; add butter, salt and pepper. Mix flour with a one third cup of cold water and stir into hot liquid. Add mushrooms and cook until thickened. Pour over fish casserole.

WARREN'S SOUTHERN JAMBALAYA
Mrs. Christine Warren

INGREDIENTS:

- 3 dozen large oysters
- 1 ½ pounds of diced ham
    or 3 cups of diced chicken
- 1 large onion
- 2 bay leaves, chopped
- 2 cups of long grain rice
- 8 cups of chicken or turkey stock
- 1 chopped bell pepper
- 2 cloves of garlic, minced
- 2 cups of chopped celery
- Salt, pepper, parsley

DIRECTIONS:

Fry onions, celery, bell pepper, garlic in fat until brown. Add ham, turkey, oysters, and shrimp. Cook for 20 minutes. Add turkey stock; Add rice, cover and cook for 40 minutes. Serves 12–14. IMPORTANT: Do not stir. Serve with a mixed green salad, tinted apples, and French bread.

• •

OYSTERS a la POULETTE
Mrs. Julia Duncan

INGREDIENTS:

- 3 dozen oysters
- 1 cup of boiled, peeled shrimp
- 3 egg yolks
- 3 tablespoons of cooking oil
- 4 teaspoons of flour (heaping)
- 4 teaspoons of butter
- 3 teaspoons of lemon juice
- 1 cup of milk
- 1 teaspoon of Worcestershire sauce
- 1 cup of oyster water
- 1 teaspoon of paprika
- ½ teaspoon of finely chopped garlic
- 1 teaspoon of chopped green pepper
- Salt and pepper to taste

DIRECTIONS:

Place oil and butter in a saucepan over a lot of heat. Add flour then oysters and all other ingredients. Cook on low heat for 15 minutes. Just before serving, beat egg yolks, stir into mixture. Cook a few minutes longer. Serve in pastry shells.

CAWAIN (Soft Shell Turtle Stew)
Mrs. Ella Rieras

INGREDIENTS:

- 4 pounds of cleaned turtle meat
- 2 tablespoons of flour
- 2 tablespoons of cooking oil
- 1 large can of whole tomatoes
- 1 bay leaf
- 1 large onion
- 1 sprig thyme
- 5 cloves of garlic, minced
- 1 tablespoon of chopped parsley
- Salt, cayenne pepper to taste
- ½ lemon

DIRECTIONS:

Steam turtle meat for 30 minutes. Drain thoroughly. Take 2 tablespoons of flour and 2 tablespoons of cooking oil, mix, and brown. Add 1 large onion, 5 cloves of garlic, brown all. Then add can of tomatoes. Let this fry for about 10 minutes on low fire. Add turtle meat, bay leaf, thyme, salt, and pepper. Add 3 cups of water, 1 tablespoon of chopped parsley, and half of a lemon. Simmer until tender. Serves 6.

OIGNONS GLACES (Glazed Onions)
Mildred Hastings Swerdlow

INGREDIENTS:

- 1 ½ dozen small onions of uniform size
- 1 tablespoon of brown sugar
- 1 cup of water
- 1 large teaspoon of butter
- Salt to taste

DIRECTIONS:

Select small Creole onions of uniform size, remove the first skin. Take an oven proof dish large enough for the onions to be placed side by side without crowding. Place butter in dish, heat; when the butter has melted add the onions. Sprinkle with the sugar and the water. When nearly done (about 45 minutes) and tender, add a tablespoonful of cornstarch or flour, mixed in water; blend well. Cover dish with paper foil and let stand for about one hour in the oven. The onions will be nicely glazed and will make a wonderful garnish for any meat dish.

SHRIMP CREOLE
Mrs. Juliet Walker-Mitchell

INGREDIENTS:

- 2 pounds of shrimp
- 2 cups of cooked or canned tomatoes
- 1 green Creole sweet pepper
- 2 tablespoons of butter
- 1 medium onion, chopped
- 2 tablespoons of flour
- 1 celery stalk, chopped
- 1 teaspoon of salt
- 1 bay leaf
- 1 sprig of thyme
- 1 teaspoon of Worcestershire sauce
- ½ teaspoon of sugar

DIRECTIONS:

Melt butter over low flame. Add onions, fry until limp but not brown. Push onion to one side; add flour, blend until brown. Add tomatoes, minced pepper, celery, bay leaf, thyme, Worcestershire sauce, sugar, and salt. Cook over low flame, stirring constantly until thickened. Let simmer for 20 minutes. Boil shrimp and remove shells, devein, sauté in melted butter for 5 minutes and add to above sauce. Serve with fluffy rice.

 Canned shrimp was offered as a substitute for fresh shrimp in this recipe.

SHRIMP BALLS
Mrs. Ernest Cherrie

INGREDIENTS:

- 1 pound of shrimp
- ½ loaf of stale bread
- 1 large onion, chopped
- 2 eggs
- 4 cloves of garlic, minced
- ¼ cup of chopped parsley
- 2 tablespoons of fat
- Salt and pepper to taste

DIRECTIONS:

Sauté chopped onion and garlic until tender. Add sufficient water to bread to soften. Add onion, garlic, and chopped shrimp to bread. Beat eggs and add to mixture. Blend well. Shape into balls and fry in deep fat.

SHRIMP REMOULADE
Mrs. Daisy Hatter

INGREDIENTS:

- 1 small garlic clove, minced
- 2 tablespoons of cider vinegar
- 1 raw egg yolk
- 3 tablespoons of salad oil
- ½ teaspoon of dry mustard
- 1 can of chopped anchovies
- 2 hard (boiled) cooked eggs
- ½ cup of finely chopped celery
- Juice of ½ lemon
- 1 pound of shrimp, cooked

DIRECTIONS:

Make a paste of salt and garlic by crushing together. Blend raw egg yolk, mustard, yolks of cooked eggs, and garlic paste. Add lemon juice, vinegar, and oil. Beat until thick. Stir in chopped egg whites, anchovies, and celery. Add salt and cayenne pepper. Pour over shrimp, toss. Chill for at least 1 hour. Serve on lettuce.

 May also be served as a cocktail.

GRILLADES
Mrs. Lydia G. Sindos

INGREDIENTS:

- 2 or 3 veal shoulder pounds, or "7" steaks
- 1 small or ¼ large bell pepper, chopped
- 1 small sprig of thyme
- 1 small hot green pepper minced (optional)
- 1 tablespoon of chopped parsley
- 1 cup of freshly sliced or canned tomatoes or 2 tablespoons of tomato paste
- 1 ½ cups of water

DIRECTIONS:

Cut into wedges 2 or 3 veal shoulder pounds, or "7" steaks. Season with salt and black pepper. Brown lightly in hot oil. Remove from oil and let drain on paper towels. Pour off excess oil; make a roux with flour, brown well. Let boil briskly for 10 minutes. Add meat, simmer until meat is tender and gravy is the consistency desired.

GUMBO Z'HERBES
Mrs. Ernest Cherrie

INGREDIENTS:

- 1 bunch of spinach
- 1 bunch of watercress
- 1 bunch of turnip greens
- 1 bunch of beet greens
- 1 bunch of collard greens
- 1 bunch of mustard greens
- 1 green cabbage
- 1 large sliced ham, chopped
- 1 large sliced pickle meat
- 1 pound of hot sausage, chopped
- 1 onion, chopped
- 1 garlic clove, chopped
- Salt and pepper to taste

DIRECTIONS:

Parboil greens until tender. Chop fine. Fry chopped meats with onions and garlic. When brown, add greens and simmer for about 30 minutes.

CREOLE GUMBO WITH OKRA
Mrs. August Terrence

INGREDIENTS:

- 1 ½ pounds of okra
- 1 ½ pounds of shrimp
- 1 sliced ham, chopped
- ½ dozen crabs
- 1 large onion
- 2 cloves of garlic, minced
- ½ green pepper, chopped
- 2 tomatoes, chopped
- 2 tablespoons of cooking oil

DIRECTIONS:

Wash and drain okra and cut into slices. Place oil in a skillet, add okra and brown slowly. Add peeled shrimp, ham and tomatoes. Sauté slowly. Scald and clean crabs. Place all ingredients in a pot with 2 quarts of water. Simmer an hour or until slightly thickened.

 Filé gumbo is made in this manner with the same ingredients except chicken or leftover turkey and oysters are added, and filé is substituted for okra.

EGGPLANT WITH CRABMEAT

Mrs. Bona V. Arnaud

INGREDIENTS:

- Meat from 3 large crabs
  or 5 ounces frozen crabmeat
- 2 large eggplants
- 3 slices of stale bread,
  soaked in evaporated milk
- ¼ cup of butter or oleo
- 1 medium onion, finely chopped
- 2 tablespoons of finely chopped
  green pepper
- Salt, pepper, and buttered crumbs

DIRECTIONS:

Wash and pare eggplants. Cut in cubes. Boil in uncovered pot until tender. Force through a sieve. Melt butter in a saucepan. Add onions and sweet pepper. Sauté until soft. Add crab meat, the sieved eggplant, and milk soaked bread. Salt and pepper to taste. Pour into a casserole. Top with buttered breadcrumbs and bake in oven, 375 degrees, for about 45 minutes.

 Squash or mirlitons can be used instead of eggplant.

HOMEMADE TOMATO CATSUP (Cajun Recipe)

Phyllis Champion

INGREDIENTS:

- ½ cup of chopped tomatoes
- 1 tablespoon of cloves
- 2 large onions, chopped
- 1 tablespoon of allspice
- 8 garlic cloves, minced
- 3 pints of cider vinegar
- Salt, sugar to taste

DIRECTIONS:

Cut and core tomatoes, place in a large pot. Add chopped onions and garlic. Cook until tender. Strain. Add salt to taste and at least 1 cup of sugar. Add vinegar. Wrap spices in cheesecloth, add to tomato mixture. Allow to cook until thick, stirring occasionally.

PECAN PRALINES
Mrs. Bona V. Arnaud

INGREDIENTS:

- 1 cup of brown sugar
- 1 cup of granulated sugar
- ½ cup of evaporated milk
- 2 tablespoons of butter
- 1 ½ or 2 cups of pecans

DIRECTIONS:

Put the sugar and the evaporated milk in a saucepan. Stir until the mixture spins as a thread or makes a ball when tested in water. Add butter and nuts. Set aside to cool for 2 to 3 minutes. Then beat until mixture thickens slightly. Drop by tablespoonsful on greased, waxed paper.

• •

CREAMY CREOLE CHOCOLATE FUDGE
Mrs. Natalie Forcia

INGREDIENTS:

- 1 ½ cups of sugar
- 2 squares of bitter chocolate
- ½ cup of brown sugar
- ⅛ teaspoon of salt
- 2 tablespoons of light Karo syrup
- 2 tablespoons of butter
- ¾ cup of milk
- 1 teaspoon of vanilla
- 1 cup of chopped pecans

DIRECTIONS:

Place sugar, salt, and milk in a saucepan with finely grated chocolate. Cook over low fire, stirring constantly until all ingredients are melted. Bring to a boil and cook without stirring until a soft ball will form in cold water. Add butter and vanilla. Cool and beat until candy begins to lose its gloss. Stir in pecans and pour into a buttered pan. When cold, cut into squares.

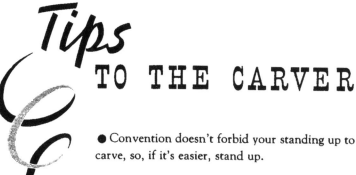

Tips TO THE CARVER

- Convention doesn't forbid your standing up to carve, so, if it's easier, stand up.

- The bones get in your way if you don't know where to expect them; a little investigation tells you just where they are.

- Carving is unduly complicated by a dull knife.

- And remember the first rule of carving . . . . .
  "Cut across the grain"
If you cut with the grain, long meat fibers give a stringy texture to the slice. Steaks are the exception.

Tips TO THE HOSTESS

- A large roast can be carved more easily after it stands for about thirty minutes.

- When garnishing, don't be over-generous; leave space for the work to be done.

- Servings cool quickly so plates and platter *must* be heated.

- An inexperienced carver will appreciate a hostess who keeps the guests' attention diverted from his carving.

Louisiana Yams Around the Clock

Pies, Cakes, Vegetables, Etc.

YAMS, from the romantic Evangeline Country, like rice, sugar cane, and citrus fruits, are native to Louisiana. Each year in Opelousas there is a Yambilee—a festival celebrating the lowly but delicious yam. For this reason, we present a variety of recipes for the fastidious gourmet, some of which are selected from a booklet prepared by the Louisiana Sweet Potato Commission.

YAM TOMATO BISQUE

INGREDIENTS:

- 3 tablespoons of bacon drippings
- ¼ cup of finely chopped onion
- ½ cup of coarsely diced green pepper
- ¼ cup of butter or margarine
- ½ cup of boiling water
- ¼ cup of all-purpose flour
- 1 teaspoon of salt
- 4 cups of milk
- 4 medium Louisiana yams, peeled and coarsely diced
- 2 ½ cups of canned tomatoes
- 1 tablespoon of brown sugar
- Salt and pepper to taste

DIRECTIONS:

Heat bacon drippings; add onion and green pepper and cook until tender. Add water, salt, and yams. Heat to boiling point over medium heat and cook covered until yams are almost tender. Add tomatoes and brown sugar; cook covered for 10 minutes.

Meanwhile, melt butter or margarine over low heat; add flour and blend. Gradually add milk and cook until thickened, stirring constantly. Add white sauce to yam mixture and season to taste with salt and pepper. Makes 6 servings.

YAM NUT MUFFINS

INGREDIENTS:

- 1 ¾ cups of sifted all-purpose flour
- 2 tablespoons of brown sugar
- 1 teaspoon of salt
- 3 teaspoons of baking powder
- ¼ cup of melted butter or margarine
- ½ cup of coarsely chopped walnuts
- 2 eggs, well beaten
- Cinnamon
- Sugar
- ½ cup of mil
- 1 ¼ cups of mashed cooked Louisiana yams, fresh or canned

DIRECTIONS:

Stir flour, salt, brown sugar, and baking powder together. Add walnuts and mix well. Combine eggs, milk, yams, and butter or margarine; mix well. Add yam mixture to dry ingredients all at once and mix only until ingredients are combined. Fill greased 2-inch muffin pans ⅔ full. Sprinkle lightly with cinnamon and sugar. Bake in hot oven, 425 degrees, 35 to 40 minutes or until done. Makes 12 2-inch muffins

LOUISIANA GRIDDLE CAKES

INGREDIENTS:

- 1 ½ cups of sifted all-purpose flour
- 3 ½ teaspoons of baking powder
- 1 teaspoon of salt
- ½ teaspoon of nutmeg
- 2 eggs, well beaten
- ¼ cup of melted butter or margarine
- 1 ½ cups of milk
- 1 ¼ cups of mashed cooked Louisiana yams, fresh or canned

DIRECTIONS:

Sift flour, baking powder, salt and nutmeg together. Combine remaining ingredients and mix well. Add to dry ingredients and mix only until ingredients are blended. Drop by spoonfuls on a hot griddle. Bake on both sides until browned. Serve with butter and jelly or syrup, as desired. Makes 4 servings.

· ·

ORANGE SWEET POTATOES

Mrs. Margaret Colteryahn (Pittsburgh, PA)

INGREDIENTS:

- 6 medium sweet potatoes
- 3 tablespoons of melted butter or oleo
- 1 cup of orange juice
- ⅓ cup of brown sugar
- 2 teaspoons of grated orange rind
- ⅓ cup of white sugar
- 1 tablespoon of cornstarch
- Pinch of salt

DIRECTIONS:

Boil potatoes with jackets until nearly done. Peel and cut in halves or thick slices. Arrange in a greased shallow baking dish. Combine remaining ingredients, cook, stirring until thickened. Pour over potatoes and bake in a moderate oven, 350 degrees, for about 30 or 35 minutes.

MINTED YAM AND PINEAPPLE BAKE

INGREDIENTS:

- 2 cups of canned crush pineapple
- 1 tablespoon of cornstarch
- 3 tablespoons of butter or margarine
- Green food coloring
- 6 to 8 medium Louisiana yams, cooked and peeled
- Fresh or canned mint extract

DIRECTIONS:

Drain ¼ cup of pineapple syrup from pineapple; heat remaining pineapple and syrup to boiling point. Combine ¼ cup of pineapple syrup with cornstarch and mix well. Add to hot pineapple and cook over low heat, stirring constantly until thickened. Add butter or margarine and mint extract to taste. Tint sauce a light green with coloring. Cut yams in half crosswise and place greased shallow casserole. Pour mint sauce over yams. Cover and bake in a slow oven, 325 degrees, 25 to 30 minutes. Makes 6 servings.

. . . .

BAKED STUFFED YAMS WITH BRANDY

INGREDIENTS:

- 6 baked Louisiana yams
- ¼ cup of butter
- ½ teaspoon of salt
- ½ cup of brown sugar, firmly packed
- ½ cup of chopped peanuts
- Dash of nutmeg
- ½ cup of brandy

DIRECTIONS:

Slice off small portion of each yam and scoop pulp into a mixing bowl. Blend with butter, sugar, brandy, and nuts, reserving a few nuts for the top. Whip until fluffy; pile lightly back into shells. Return to a hot oven, 450 degrees, about 10 minutes before serving. Makes 6 serving.

SWEET POTATO PIE

Mrs. Charles S. Johnson (Nashville, TN)

BLEND WELL:

- 6 tablespoons of brown sugar
- 2 tablespoons of white sugar
- ½ teaspoon of salt
- 1 teaspoon of cinnamon
- ½ teaspoon of ginger
- ⅛ teaspoon of cloves
- ½ cup of dark corn syrup
- 3 slightly beaten eggs

The egg whites may be beaten separately and folded in last. Add:

- 1 ½ cooked sweet potatoes
- 1 ½ cups of undiluted evaporated milk or rich cream
- 1 teaspoon of vanilla

DIRECTIONS:

Line a 9-inch pie pan with pie crust. Build up a high fluted edge. Pour the sweet potato pie mixture into the pie shell. Bake the pie in a hot oven, 425 degrees, for about 1 hour or until a silver knife inserted in the filling comes out clean.

• •

YAM COCONUT PIE

INGREDIENTS:

- 1 ¼ cups of mashed cooked Louisiana yams, fresh or canned
- 1 cup of toasted shredded coconut
- ½ cup of chopped peanuts
- 3 eggs, beaten
- 2 cups of milk
- ¼ cup of sugar
- 1 unbaked 9-inch pastry shell
- ½ teaspoon of salt

DIRECTIONS:

Combine yams and eggs; beat well. Add sugar, salt, coconut, and peanuts; mix well. Add milk and mix well. Turn into pastry shell. Bake in a hot oven, 400 degrees, 1 hour until a knife inserted in the center comes out clean. Cool thoroughly. Top with meringue, if desired.

For Meringue: Beat 3 egg whites with ⅛ teaspoon of cream of tartar and a dash of salt until frothy. Gradually add 6 tablespoons of sugar, one tablespoon at a time, beating constantly. Beat until stiff. Spread meringue over yam filling. Bake in slow oven (325 degrees) 20 minutes or until meringue is lightly browned. Makes a 9-inch pie.

SWEET POTATO PUDDING

INGREDIENTS:

- 4 large sweet potatoes
- Grated skin of 1 lemon and 1 orange
- 1 cup of molasses
- ½ teaspoon of ground cloves
- 1 cup of brown sugar
- ½ teaspoon of ground cinnamon
- 1 cup of milk
- 4 eggs
- 1 cup of butter

DIRECTIONS:

Grate the potatoes. Beat butter and sugar until creamy; add well beaten eggs, and blend well. Add grated potato, spices and milk. Beat all well together; add the grated lemon and orange skins. Pour mixture in a well buttered pan and bake slowly for about an hour. It may be served hot or cold cut into slices. It is delicious when served at luncheon cold with a glass of fresh milk.

· ·

YAM APRICOT SHERBET

INGREDIENTS:

- 1 ¼ cups of mashed cooked Louisiana yams, fresh or canned
- ¼ cup of white corn syrup
- ⅛ teaspoon of salt
- 1 egg white, stiffly beaten
- 1 cup of pureed apricots
- 2 cups of milk
- ⅓ cup of lemon juice
- ½ cup of sugar

DIRECTIONS:

Combine yams, apricots, lemon juice, sugar, corn syrup, and salt. Mix well. Fold in egg white. Gradually stir yam mixture into milk; mix until thoroughly blended. Turn into refrigerator trays and freeze until frozen 1 inch from sides of tray. Turn into bowl and beat with rotary beater or electric mixer until light and fluffy. Pour into refrigerator trays. Freeze until firm.

Appetizers, Pickles, and Relish

AVOCADO DIP
Mrs. Tibbye Thomas

INGREDIENTS:

- 1 avocado, mashed
- 2 tablespoons of lemon juice
- 2 teaspoons of onion, chopped fine
- ½ cup of cream cheese
- Dash of Worcestershire sauce
- Salt and pepper to taste

DIRECTIONS:

Peel avocado and mash. Add the other ingredients and blend thoroughly. Chill. Serve with potato chips, Fritos, or cheese puffs.

· ·

CHEESE PUFFS
Grace Lepine

INGREDIENTS:

- ½ pound of cheese
- 1 cup of flour
- ¼ pound of butter
- ½ teaspoon of salt
- ¼ teaspoon of cayenne pepper

DIRECTIONS:

Grate cheese, mix all ingredients until smooth, forming a round ball. Pinch off small pieces and roll into a marble sized ball. Place on an ungreased baking sheet. Bake in 350 degree oven 20–25 minutes. Chopped olives or toasted nuts may be added to the ingredients.

· ·

CHOPPED LIVER (Gehakte Leber)
Mrs. Charles Swerdlow (Phoenix, AZ)

INGREDIENTS:

- 1 pound of liver
    (beef, calf, chicken, or goose)
- 2 hard boiled eggs
- Salt and pepper to taste
- 1 onion, chopped
- 2 tablespoons of schmaltz (or butter)

DIRECTIONS:

Place liver under broiler and broil until well done (about 10 minutes), turning once. Remove from broiler and cool. Remove skin and veins. Put liver, eggs, and onion through a food grinder, using the fine blade. Season with salt and pepper. Add schmaltz, working it through the liver with a fork. The liver should be moist enough to hold together; if necessary, add more schmaltz. Serve on toasted bread rounds. Serves 8.

EGG CUSHIONS
Mrs. I. M. Mitchell

INGREDIENTS:

- 6 hard boiled eggs
- 24 small rounds of bread
- 2-ounce can of caviar
- Paprika
- ½ cup of mayonnaise
- Granulated parsley

DIRECTIONS:

Pass egg yolks through a fine strainer. Place a small portion of caviar on 12 rounds of bread. Cover with other 12 rounds to form small sandwiches. Cover sandwiches with mayonnaise, top and sides. Roll in strained egg yolk. Sprinkle with granulated parsley and paprika. Makes 12.

• •

WATERMELON PICKLES
Mrs. Floyd Morgan

INGREDIENTS:

- 7 pounds of watermelon rind
- ½ cup of water
- 3 ½ pounds of sugar (7 cups)
- ½ teaspoon of oil of cinnamon
- 1 ½ cups of vinegar
- ½ teaspoon of clove

DIRECTIONS:

Cover rinds with hot water and parbroil until they are a little tender. (Don't soak overnight.) Drain well for four hours. Bring a solution of vinegar and sugar to a boil and add a rind and boil for 15 minutes. Let stand for 24 hours and boil again. On the third day bring to a boil, add cinnamon and cloves before packing and sealing.

• •

RED PEPPER JAM
Miss Helen Albro (Atlanta, GA)

INGREDIENTS:

- 12 sweet red peppers
- 3 cups of sugar
- 2 cups of vinegar
- 1 tablespoon of salt

DIRECTIONS:

Remove stems and seeds from peppers and chop fine. Mix in salt and let stand for 3 hours. Drain well. Add sugar and vinegar and then cook slowly until like jam. Put in hot jars and cover with paraffin. Note: Delicious relish for roast beef.

SCAMPI
Mrs. Lucile Segre

INGREDIENTS:

- 2 pounds of raw shrimp (fresh or frozen)
- ½ pound of butter or margarine
- Salt and pepper
- 1 clove of garlic, minced fine

DIRECTIONS:

Shell and devein shrimp, trying to keep the tails intact. Melt butter, add garlic, and simmer for 3 minutes. Place the shrimp on individual flame-proof platters, on a large broiling pan or on heavy aluminum foil with the edges turned up. Pour garlic butter over shrimp. Sprinkle with salt and pepper. Place in a pre-heated broiler 4 inches from heat and broil 5 to 10 minutes or until brown and tender. Do not overcook. Makes 4 to 6 servings. Serve on toothpicks or toast wedges.

. . . .

WELSH RAREBIT
Grace Lepin

INGREDIENTS:

- 1 pound of cheddar cheese, grated
- ½ cup of mayonnaise
- ¼ cup of cream
- ¼ cup of Worcestershire sauce
- ½ cup of stale beer

DIRECTIONS:

Blend mayonnaise and cream together in a double broiler. Add cheese, Worchestire sauce and beer, stirring until cheese melts. Serve with crackers or Melba toast.

Soups,
Salads,
Sauces,
Dressings

COLD VEGETABLE SOUP
Mrs. Claire Harvey (Jackson, MS)

INGREDIENTS:

- 1 can of tomato soup
- Juice from 1 can of beets
- 3–4 tablespoons of tarragon vinegar

DIRECTIONS:

Pour together tomato soup, beet juice, and tarragon vinegar. Shake vigorously in a covered jar or whip with an electric mixer. Garnish with unpeeled cucumber slices before serving.

FISH CHOWDER
Mrs. William N. Davis

INGREDIENTS:

- ¼ pound of salt pork
- 2 teaspoons of salt
- 1 cup of sliced onions
- ¼ teaspoon of pepper
- 1 ½ pounds of cod fillets
- 2 cups of boiling water
- 5 medium sliced potatoes
- 4 cups of milk

DIRECTIONS:

Cut salt pork into ½-inch cubes; brown well in a large kettle. Add onions and cook until tender. Cut fish into small pieces. Add fish, potatoes, water, and seasonings to kettle. Cover and simmer for 25 minutes. Add milk, heat, and serve with crackers.

VICHYSOISSE
Ebony Test Kitchen

INGREDIENTS:

- 8 small raw potatoes
- 1 pint of chicken stock or soup
- 2 onions, chopped
- 1 teaspoon of salt
- 1 tablespoon of butter
- ½ teaspoon of pepper
- 1 pint of heavy cream

DIRECTIONS:

Peel and cook potatoes until tender. Drain off water and cool. Mash to a pulp. Place chicken stock and potato water in a pan. Simmer for 15 to 20 minutes with sautéed onions and butter. Add cream. Let stand. Chill and service iced.

AVOCADO WITH LOBSTER
Mrs. Lucile Segre

INGREDIENTS:

- 3 medium avocados
- 2 green onions, chopped
- 1 teaspoon of lemon juice
- 1 teaspoon of Worcestershire sauce
- 1 can of lobster
- 2 hard boiled eggs, chopped
- 1 cup of minced celery
- ½ cup of mayonnaise

DIRECTIONS:

Peel avocados, cut in half, remove seed, rub surface with lemon juice. Break up lobster into chunks; mix with celery, onions, Worcestershire sauce, egg, and mayonnaise. Stuff into cavity of avocados. Place on a crisp shredded lettuce (bed), garnish with sliced tomatoes sprinkled with French dressing. Serve with mayonnaise to which has been added 2 tablespoons of tomato paste and finely chopped olives.

· ·

AVOCADO AND SHRIMP SALAD
Mildred Hastings Swerdlow

INGREDIENTS:

- 2 pounds of chilled broiled shrimp
- 2 medium size avocados
- French dressing
- 1 can of Supreme olives

DIRECTIONS:

Boil shrimp in salted water to which several bay leaves and 1 teaspoon of red pepper has been added. Clean and cut in half; chill thoroughly. An hour before serving cut the avocado into cubes, reserving one avocado for garnishing. Slice olives, toss together with French dressing in a wooden bowl with silver fork (to prevent discoloring). Allow mixture to season in bowl before serving on glass salad plates with purple cabbage leaves instead of lettuce. The contrast in colors makes the salad very attractive. Serve with cheese sticks.

CHICKEN ROYAL SALAD
Mrs. Irene Waters

INGREDIENTS:

- 1 cup of cooked chicken or turkey
- 2 tablespoons of French dressing
- 1 small ripe tomato, chopped
- 1 envelope of gelatin
- ¼ cup of chopped green pepper
- 1 can of cream celery soup

DIRECTIONS:

Soften gelatin in ½ cup of cold water. Place in top of double boiler, heat until gelatin is dissolved. Blend in soup and remaining ½ cup of water. Refrigerate until slightly thickened. Fold in mixed chopped chicken, tomato, green pepper, French dressing, and black pepper. Pour into quart mold. Chill until firm. Serve on crisp salad green. Serves 4.

ENTRÉE
Mrs. Carrie Johnson (Atlanta, GA)

INGREDIENTS:

- 3 grapefruits
- 1 avocado
- 1 pound of shrimp
- 1 lime
- French dressing
- 1 lemon

DIRECTIONS:

Cut 3 grapefruits in half. Remove centers and separate sections. Add a small amount of sugar to each grapefruit half. Marinate cooked shrimp in French dressing overnight. Dice 1 large avocado and pour over it the juice of the lemon and lime. Mix shrimp and avocado and pile on grapefruit halves. Garnish with a sprig of parsley.

PINEAPPLE COTTAGE CHEESE SALAD
Mrs. Jesse O. Richards

INGREDIENTS:

- 1 package (3 ounces) of lime gelatin
- ½ cup of mayonnaise
- 1 ¼ cups of hot water
- 1 cup of dry cottage cheese
- 2 tablespoons of horseradish
- 1 No. 2 can of crushed pineapple, drained

DIRECTIONS:

Dissolve gelatin in hot water, chill, and fold in other ingredients. Place in a mold until set. Unmold on a platter with lettuce or other greens.

SEAFOOD MOLD

Mrs. Edith Brooks (Los Angeles, CA)

INGREDIENTS:

- 1 can of tomato soup
- 1 small onion, chopped
- 1 package of cream cheese
- 1 cup of mayonnaise
- ½ cup of cold water
- 3 cups of crab meat (shrimp or lobster)
- 1 cup of chopped celery
- Worcestershire sauce
- 1 ½ cups of chopped green pepper
- Tabasco sauce

DIRECTIONS:

Put tomato soup and cream cheese into a double boiler. Mix gelatin with cold water. When dissolved mix with chopped vegetables and mayonnaise. Season with Worcestershire and Tabasco sauce. Add seafood. Add this mixture to hot soup and cream cheese. Pour into large fish mold or individual molds. When congealed, unmold on lettuce, garnish with parsley, whole shrimp, and sliced hard boiled eggs.

. . . .

FRUIT AND VEGETABLE SALAD

Essie Williams

INGREDIENTS:

- 1 cup of crushed pineapples
- ½ cup of raw grated carrot
- ½ cup of celery, finely chopped
- 1 package of Jello
- 1 ½ cups of boiling water

DIRECTIONS:

Drain pineapple, chop celery, grate carrots, and combine. Mix Jello with water, allow to cool. Add fruit and vegetables. Pour into individual molds, place in refrigerator until congealed. Serve on crisp lettuce with creamed mayonnaise. Serves 6.

. . . .

BUTTERSCOTCH SAUCE (For ice cream, puddings, custards)

Mrs. J. Colomb

INGREDIENTS:

- ½ cup of sweet cream
- ¼ cup of butter
- 1 cup of dark brown sugar
- ½ cup of white Karo syrup
- 2 teaspoons of vanilla

DIRECTIONS:

Put brown sugar, syrup, and butter in a saucepan. Bring to a boil, allow to simmer until a little soft ball will form in cold water. Remove from fire, add cream, one tablespoonful at a time. Add vanilla. Place in a glass jar. This sauce will keep two to three weeks in a refrigerator.

FRENCH CHILI SAUCE

Mrs. Alice Jones Tull (Jefferson City, MO)

INGREDIENTS:

- 12 large ripe tomatoes
- 12 large apples
- 3 cups of sugar
- 9 medium onions
- 3 cups of vinegar
- 1 teaspoon of cinnamon
- 1 teaspoon of cloves
- 1 teaspoon of mustard or ginger
- 2 tablespoons of salt
- 1 tablespoon of black pepper

DIRECTIONS:

Cook together tomatoes, apples, and onions. Put through food press or sieve. Add remaining ingredients. Cook until well blended.

GREEN SAUCE FOR FISH AND SEAFOOD (French)

Geddes Jones (Paris, France)

INGREDIENTS:

- 50 grams of spinach
- 50 grams of watercress
- Curley lettuce
- 50 grams of parsley
- Fine herbs

DIRECTIONS:

Place into boiling water and keep at a rapid boil for 5 minutes; 50 grams of spinach, as much watercress, 50 grams of parsley, curley lettuce, and fine herbs. Drain and chill rapidly. Bunch leaves into a napkin and squeeze strongly in order to obtain a thick juice. Add this liquid to mayonnaise and a few chopped pickles. Season highly.

FRENCH DRESSING

Mrs. Vivian Green

INGREDIENTS:

- 3 tablespoons of catsup
- 1 teaspoon of French mustard
- 1 tablespoon of Worcestershire sauce
- ¾ cup of vinegar
- 1 tablespoon of sugar
- 1 cup of oil
- 1 tablespoon of salt

DIRECTIONS:

Mix all ingredients and shake vigorously.

OYSTER SAUCE (For steamed Red Snapper)

Jessie C. Dent

INGREDIENTS:

- 1 stick of butter
- 2 stalks of celery
- 1 onion, chopped
- ¼ cup of flour
- 1 cup of seasoned water from steamed fish or boiled shrimp
- 1 pint of oysters
- Salt and pepper to taste

DIRECTIONS:

Sauté chopped onion and celery in butter but do not brown. Add flour, then seasoned water from fish or boiled shrimp and oyster water to make 1 ½ cups of liquid. As sauce thickens, add oysters. Simmer for 5 minutes over low heat. A dash of garlic salt, onion salt, and cayenne pepper will intensify the flavor. Serve over hot steamed red snapper that has been skinned and boned.

- -

CORNISH HEN SAUCE (For basting)

Ebony Test Kitchen

INGREDIENTS:

- ¼ cup of butter
- ½ cup of dry white wine
- ½ cup of currant jelly
- 1 teaspoon of mustard
- ½ cup of pineapple juice or juice of 1 orange
- 1 teaspoon of salt
- 1 teaspoon of paprika

DIRECTIONS:

Melt ¼ pound of butter in a skillet over low heat. Add ½ cup of white dry wine. Bring to a boil. Add to butter and wine mixture ½ cup of glass currant jelly, juice from an orange (½ cup of pineapple juice may be used), blending well with each addition. Add 1 teaspoon of salt, 1 teaspoon of paprika, 1 teaspoon of dry mustard. Let boil for 5 minutes and then remove from the fire. After sauce has cooled, baste hens before placing them in a preheated oven.

Salads and salad dressings

For Appeal To The Appetite

Chill ingredients before mixing—except for molded salads.

Provide tartness in the body of salad or dressing.

Use salad greens other than lettuce sometimes. Have you tried chicory, escarole, endive, kale, spinach, dandelion greens, romaine, watercress, and chinese cabbage?

Sprinkle orange, lemon, lime, or pineapple juice on fruits that may turn dark—apples, peaches, and bananas, for instance.

For tossed green salads, tear greens in fairly large pieces or cut with scissors. Larger pieces give more body to the salad.

Prevent wilting and sogginess by drying the greens used in salads, draining canned foods well before adding to salad, using just enough salad dressing to moisten. For raw vegetable salads, add dressing at the last minute.

Fruit Combinations

1. Sliced pineapple, apricot halves, sweet red cherries.
2. Watermelon balls, peach slices, orange slices.
3. Grapefruit sections, banana slices, berries or cherries.
4. Grapefruit sections, unpared apple slices.
5. Peach slices, pear slices, halves of red plums.
6. Pineapple wedges, banana slices, strawberries.
7. Cooked dried fruit, white cherries, red raspberries.

Fruit and Vegetable Combinations

1. Shredded raw carrots, diced apples, raisins.
2. Sliced or ground cranberries, diced celery and apples, orange sections.
3. Thin cucumber slices, pineapple cubes.
4. Avocado and grapefruit sections, tomato slices.
5. Shredded cabbage, orange sections, crushed pineapple.

Vegetable Combinations

1. Grated carrots, diced celery, cucumber slices.
2. Spinach, endive, or lettuce, with tomato wedges.
3. Sliced raw cauliflower flowerets, chopped green pepper, celery, pimiento.
4. Shredded cabbage, cucumber cubes, slivers of celery.
5. Cubed cooked beets, thinly sliced celery, sweet onions.
6. Cooked whole-kernel corn and shredded snap beans, sweet pickles, onion rings.

MAIN DISHES

Meat, Sea Food, Poultry

ANYBODY'S STEW
Alvin S. Bynum

INGREDIENTS:

- 1 ½ pounds bone-in stew meat
- 6 medium potatoes, quartered
- 4 carrots, sliced
- 2 medium onions, coarsely chopped
- ½ cup of chopped celery
- 1 small whole apple
- ½ small sweet pepper, chopped
- 1 tablespoon of parsley, chopped
- 1 cup of tomato sauce or catsup
- 1 garlic clove, whole
- ¼ teaspoon of black pepper
- Dash of Worcestershire sauce (optional)
- 1 teaspoon of sugar
- 1 small can of sautéed mushrooms
- ½ cup of cooking sherry or sauterne
- Salt

DIRECTIONS:

Braise meat in stew pot with a small amount of fat. Add onions, celery, and parsley and cook until soft. Add other ingredients, plus water to cover and bring to a boil. Cover and simmer until potatoes are tender, adding enough water to keep from sticking. Serve with green salad and French bread. Serves 4.

. . . .

STUFFED HAM
Mrs. Harriet Holmes

INGREDIENTS:

- 15-pound ham
- 1 cup of white sugar
- 1 jar of India relish
- 1 cup of brown sugar
- 1 jar of mustard chow-chow
- 1 grated onion
- ½ cup of celery seed
- 1 bunch of parsley, chopped
- 4 teaspoons of dry mustard
- 1 pound of unsalted crackers
- 1 teaspoon of black pepper

DIRECTIONS:

Toast crackers; roll into fine crumbs. Mix all ingredients except brown sugar. Fill cavity of boned ham with mixture. Pat remaining mixture over the top of the ham. Cover with brown sugar. Place in a moderate oven, 350 degrees, for 2 hours. Decorate with slices of lemon and cloves.

BAKED PIG
Mrs. Anita Gilbert

INGREDIENTS:

- 18–20-pound pig, dressed
- 8 cloves of garlic or garlic salt
- 1 stalk of celery, chopped
- 2 sprigs of thyme
- 3 large onions, chopped
- 2 hot peppers
- 1 large bell pepper
- 1 bunch of green onions
- 2 bay leaves
- ½ bunch of parsley, chopped
- Salt

DIRECTIONS:

Wash pig thoroughly. Rub outside with salt, pepper, and garlic salt. Chop all other ingredients. Mix well, and use as stuffing for the pig. Fasten the pig together with skewers, wrap in foil, bake in a slow oven for 250 degrees, from 5 to 6 hours. Remove foil during the last hour of baking. Raise the temperature to 450 degrees. Bake until golden brown. Fasten the apple in the mouth with skewers.

PORK CHOPS WITH OYSTER STUFFING
Mrs. P. Q. Yancy (Atlanta, GA)

INGREDIENTS:

- 6 loin chops, 1 or ½-inch thick
- Salt and pepper

Stuffing:

- 1 cup of grated breadcrumbs
  or 3 bread slices, soaked in milk
- 2 cloves of garlic,
  peeled and finely chopped
- 1 medium sized onion, minced
- 1 cup of minced celery
- 2 tablespoons of butter
- 1 pint of oysters
- ½ teaspoon of thyme
- Salt and pepper to taste

DIRECTIONS:

Have a butcher slit a pocket in the chops large enough to hold the stuffing. Season with salt and pepper and brown slowly in a heavy frying pan. Be sure the meat is thoroughly cooked. Place stuffing in the pocket of the chops and fasten with toothpicks. Before serving, cover and slowly heat in a frying pan. Yield: 6 portions.

For Stuffing: Drop drained oysters in boiling water and allow to remain boiling until oysters curl (about 5 minutes). Drain and cool. Then cut into small pieces. Heat butter in a skillet and sauté onions and celery until lightly browned. Add garlic, adding more butter if necessary. Add all remaining ingredients (oysters, bread, and seasonings). Simmer over low heat until well mixed and ingredients are well heated.

SOUR RABBIT (Or Hasenpfeffer)

Mrs. Margaret Colteryahn (Pittsburgh, PA)

INGREDIENTS:

- 1–3 pounds rabbit
- ½ cup of vinegar
- 2 bay leaves
- ¾ cup of cold water
- A few cloves
- Salt, pepper, flour

DIRECTIONS:

Wash and dry a cleaned rabbit. Dredge with flour, salt, and pepper. Brown in hot fat. Add bay leaves, cloves, vinegar, and water. Cover and simmer until tender. Serves 4. Vinegar may be omitted.

· ·

DEVILED LOBSTER

Mrs. Christine Warren

INGREDIENTS:

- 2 cups of diced cooked lobster
- 2 tablespoons of butter
- 1 cup of soft breadcrumbs
- 2 tablespoons of flour
- 2 hard cooked eggs
- 2 cups of milk
- 2 teaspoons of lemon juice
- 1 teaspoon of salt
- ¼ teaspoon of cayenne pepper
- 1 teaspoon of anchovy paste

DIRECTIONS:

Blend lobster, crumbs, and finely chopped eggs in a saucepan. Melt butter, blend in flour, add milk, and cook until thick. Add salt, pepper, anchovy paste. Mix in lobster mixture. Pour into a greased casserole dish. Sprinkle with breadcrumbs and brown in a 350 degree oven for 15 minutes. Serves 8.

CREAMED OYSTERS
Mrs. M. S. Davage

INGREDIENTS:

- 1 pint of oysters
- 2 egg yolks
- 4 teaspoons of butter
- ½ teaspoon of salt
- 4 teaspoons of flour
- 1 teaspoon of onion juice
- ½ cup of oyster liquid
- 1 ½ cups of milk

DIRECTIONS:

Drain oysters, pick free of shells, and heat in a shallow pan or pot until edges curl. Add liquid in a pot to liquid drained oysters, add milk. Melt butter in top of a double broiler, blend in flour. Add oyster and milk mixture to blended butter and flour. Cook until thickened, stirring constantly. Add slightly beaten egg yolks and mix quickly. Add remaining ingredients; cook for 2 minutes. Serve at once on buttered toast.

CHATTER EBON'
Ebony Test Kitchen

INGREDIENTS:

- 2 pounds of raw shrimp (cleaned and cut in half lengthwise)
- 1 can of bamboo shoots, sliced
- 1 can of button mushrooms
- 4 large peeled fresh tomatoes (sliced in quarters)
- 1 large onion, sliced thin
- 1 celery stalk, sliced thin
- 1 pound of peas, fresh or frozen
- 2 cloves of garlic, minced
- ½ cup of toasted almonds, cut
- 1 small can of water chestnuts, sliced thin
- ¼ cup of salad oil or butter
- 4 cups of chicken broth
- 1 tablespoon of salt
- 1 tablespoon of paprika
- 1 tablespoon of Accent

DIRECTIONS:

Sauté garlic in oil. Add shrimp, onions, and celery and cook for 10 minutes. Add mushrooms, chestnuts, bamboo shoots, chicken broth, and peas. Cover and let cook for 15 minutes. Mix 3 tablespoons of cornstarch or flour with ½ cup of mushroom juice. Add to broth mixture and cook until thick. Just 5 minutes before serving time, add tomato wedges and almonds, steam for 5–7 minutes. Serve with rice and pineapple.

SHRIMP AND ARTICHOKE NEWBURG
Mrs. Anita Gilbert

INGREDIENTS:

- 6 green artichokes
- 2 cups of shrimp (cooked)
- 2–3 cups of medium white sauce
- 1 lemon, diced
- ¼ cup of sherry, optional
- ¼ cup of butter
- Salt and pepper to taste

DIRECTIONS:

Boil artichokes in salted water with lemon for 1 hour or until tender. Drain and cool. Remove hearts and set aside. Remove pulp from leaves. Place pulp in a sauce pan, add butter, and simmer for about 5 minutes, stirring constantly. Stuff this mixture into artichoke hearts. Make white sauce in top of double broiler, add cooked shrimp, and heat thoroughly. Add sherry and remove from heat. Arrange stuffed hearts on a hot platter and pour shrimp mixture over. Garnish with toast wedges, parsley sprigs, and lemon. Serves 6.

GUINEA HENS
Mrs. Juliet Walker Mitchell

INGREDIENTS:

- 2–2 ½ or 3-pound guineas (frozen)
- 1 large green pepper, diced
- 1 clove of garlic, minced
- ½ cup of all-purpose flour
- ⅙-ounce can of tomato paste
- 2 teaspoons of salt
- 2 cans of water
- ¼ teaspoon of black pepper
- 1 pound of mushrooms, sliced
- 5 tablespoons of olive oil
- 1 2 ½ can of tomatoes
- 1 large onion, sliced
- ½ teaspoon of thyme
- 2 bay leaves
- Pepper to taste
- Salt to taste
- 1 cup of white wine

DIRECTIONS:

Cut defrosted guineas in quarters (stewing hen will suffice). Roll in seasoned flour and fry in four tablespoons of oil until golden brown on one side, then the other. Remove guineas from pan and place in a Dutch oven. Add 1 tablespoon of oil in a pan; add onion, pepper, and garlic and cook over low heat (about 10 minutes) or until tender; onion and garlic should be a light gold. Pour over guinea hens and simmer for about 1 ½ hours. Turn tomato paste and water into a frying pan to blend and pour over hens before simmering. Turn off heat and let the dish stand for 30 minutes before dinner. Add 1 cup of wine and heat thoroughly. Serve with wild rice, or white rice, or buttered noodles. Yields: 4 portions.

STUFFED CAPON

Mrs. Marie E. Burbridge

INGREDIENTS:

- 1 capon, 6–8 pounds
- 2 tablespoons of cooking oil
- 2 tablespoons of butter
- 4 tablespoons of flour
- Salt and pepper to taste

Oyster Dressing:

- 1 ½ cups of stale breadcrumbs
- 2 strips of bacon, chopped
- 1 ½ tablespoons of onion, chopped
- 1 dozen small oysters and liquid
- 1 garlic clove, chopped
- ¾ cup of butter or shortening
- 1 bay leaf

DIRECTIONS:

Singe capon while dry. Clean inside and cut. Wash and dry, then sprinkle inside and out with salt and pepper. Fill with oyster dressing. Sew up or close with skewers. Pour over oil and butter; place in a roaster. Bake in a hot oven, 450 degrees, until golden brown and tender.

For Oyster Dressing: Mix all ingredients well. Add melted butter and enough oyster liquid to hold mixture together.

· ·

HUNGARIAN CHICKEN PAPRIKA

Mrs. Lenora Cooper

INGREDIENTS:

- 1 large frying chicken, cut into parts
- 1 large onion
- ¼ cup of fat
- 1 cup of sliced mushrooms, drained
- 1 can of tomato soup
- 2 large bay leaves
- ½ pint of sour cream
- ½ teaspoon of salt
- 1 tablespoon of paprika
- ½ teaspoon of black pepper

DIRECTIONS:

Dust chicken in seasoned flour. In a hot fat skillet, brown chickens slightly on all sides. Remove chicken from the pan. Add minced onions, mushrooms, salt, and pepper to fat. Sauté until onions are tender. Add a can of un-diluted tomato soup, sour cream, bay leaves, and paprika. Stir. Add chicken. Simmer covered on very low flame for 45 minutes or until the chicken is fork tender. Serve with rice.

SPANISH REST

Mrs. Mable Armstrong (Wabasso, FL)

INGREDIENTS:

- ½ pound of chicken liver
- 3 tablespoons of butter
- ½ pound of onions
- ½ cup of sauterne wine or sherry
- 2 tablespoons of mushrooms, diced
- Pinch of salt and pepper

DIRECTIONS:

Chop onions fine and brown in the butter. Add chicken livers. Braise until slightly brown. Add mushrooms and wine and salt and pepper to taste. Serve on rice or toast.

DUCKLING IN ASPIC

Mrs. Mary E. Slade

INGREDIENTS:

- 6-pound duckling, cleaned and drawn
- 2 cloves
- 2 ½ teaspoons of salt
- 4 peppercorns
- Pepper to taste
- 1 bay leaf
- 1 small onion
- 2 cups of dry white wine
- 2 or 3 small carrots
- 1 or 2 pickles, sliced
- 1 or 2 pieces of celery or celery leaves
- 2 hard cooked eggs, sliced
- 1 ½ tablespoons of plain gelatin
- 1 sprig of parsley
- 2 tablespoons of vinegar

DIRECTIONS:

Rinse duckling inside and out. Season with salt and pepper. Place in a pot with onions, carrots, celery, parsley, cloves, peppercorns, and bay leaf. Add wine, vinegar, and enough water to cover the bird. Bring to a boil, then lower the heat, cover, and cook slowly until the bird is tender; remove and cut into four portions. Place on a serving dish; garnish with a pickle, egg, and carrots from the stewing kettle. Strain the stock from the kettle. Measure and add 1 tablespoon of gelatin to each 2 cups of stock. Let the gelatin soften in stock. Beat egg whites slightly; stir into gelatin and stock. Reheat to boiling; remove from the heat. Let stand until the mixture is clear and slightly thickened. Then pour it over the duckling. Chill in the refrigerator. When ready to serve, cut away extra gelatin about edges of portions and decorate with crisp greens and radish roses. When using larger birds or chicken, slice the meat for portions before pouring on gelatin mixture.

ROAST WILD DUCK (Teal or French)

Mrs. E. Lyons Baker

INGREDIENTS:

- 5 cups of breadcrumbs
- 4 teaspoons of cayenne pepper
- ½ cup of melted butter or bacon fat
- ½ cup of chopped celery
- 1 medium onion, chopped
- 1 teaspoon of salt
- 1 small clove of garlic

DIRECTIONS:

Pluck feathers from duck without pouring hot water over the feathers. Singe over a low flame. Wash duck inside and out. Brush over with melted butter or bacon fat. Season with salt and pepper. Then stuff the duck with wild rice or breadcrumb dressing. Close flap with pins and roll in flour. Bake in a hot oven, 400 degrees, for about 45 minutes to 1 hour, baste every 8 or 10 minutes with ⅓ cup of butter or bacon fat in ⅔ cup of boiling hot water. Celery, garlic, and onion may be placed around the duck for 15 minutes before roasting is complete. This will make and season the gravy.

For Breadcrumb Stuffing or Dressing: Sauté onion and celery with fat. Add breadcrumbs, moisten with hot water. Add salt, pepper, and finely chopped garlic clove. Let steam for about 5 minutes. This may be used plain or oysters or finely chopped green shrimp may be added. (Rice dressing may be made the same as the bread dressing if preferred.)

• •

ROCK CORNISH HEN WITH WILD RICE DRESSING

Coragreene Johnstone

Thaw hens. Wash and cook the wild rice for about 15 minutes (half cooked). Toss the rice with the celery onions, green pepper, pimento, salt, and pepper into the cavities of the hens. Stuff lightly with the dressing, about ⅔ full. Close the opening with the skewers or overcase the edges of the skin with coarse thread. Melt the remaining butter and brush the hens generously. Place them in an open roaster and bake in a preheated oven at 350 degrees for an hour and a half. Baste a few minutes with any butter left or with drippings in the roaster.

For Gravy: remove the hens to a hot platter, pour the drippings into a saucepan. Skim off the fat and into it place 2 tablespoons of flour, salt, and pepper to taste and brown. Stir constantly. Pour into this mixture the drippings from the hens and some hot water. Cook until the gravy thickens. Serve hot.

Oyster dressing, chestnut dressing, or mushroom dressing may be substituted for the wild rice dressing.

CURRIED CHICKEN IN PINEAPPLE SHELLS

Mildred Hastings Swerdlow

INGREDIENTS:

- ½ cup of butter
- ½ teaspoon of dry mustard
- 2 small onions, chopped
- 1 bay leaf
- 1 garlic clove, minced
- 3 cups of chicken stock
- 1 celery stalk, chopped
- 3 cups of cooked chicken
- 1 tart apple, diced
- 1 cup of milk or cream
- ½ cup of enriched flour
- 2 tablespoons of chopped chutney
- 2 teaspoons of curry powder
- 1 teaspoon of salt

DIRECTIONS:

In a saucepan melt butter and in it cook onions, garlic, celery, and apple for 8 minutes, stirring occasionally. Stir in flour mixed with curry powder, salt, and mustard and cook, stirring for 2 minutes. Add bay leaf, gradually stir in chicken stock and cook, stirring until sauce thickens. Cool over low heat for 30 minutes. Add chicken, cream, and chutney and cook for 3 minutes longer. Cut 3 small pineapples in half lengthwise and cut out the fruit, leaving a shell ½ inch thick. Add 1 cup of diced pineapple to curry sauce along with the chicken. When ready to serve, fill pineapple shells with the curried chicken and top with shredded coconut. Arrange shell on baking sheet in a 350 degree oven for 10 minutes. Serve with cooked white rice.

FRUIT OF THE BAYOU

Mrs. Daisy Young

INGREDIENTS:

- 1 pound of crab meat
- 1 pound of deveined shrimp, peeled
- 2 dozen oysters
- 1 pound of peeled deveined crayfish
- 1 pound of spaghetti, boiled and drained or 1 pound of rice, boiled and drained
- 2 cans of Campbell's cream of mushroom soup
- 5 green onions
- 3 celery stalks
- 2 garlic cloves
- Salt and red pepper to taste

DIRECTIONS:

Sauté green onions, celery (both minced fine), and garlic in butter. Add all seafood except oysters and cook for 10 minutes. Add oysters and oyster water. Add Campbell mushroom soup, cook slowly for 10 minutes longer. Season with salt and pepper. Make a ring of the boiled spaghetti or rice and serve fruit of the bayou in the center. This makes a beautiful party dish.

COLD FISH PLATTER
Harriette Holmes

INGREDIENTS:

- 5 pounds of redfish
- ½ lemon
- 1 sprig of thyme
- 1 teaspoon of cayenne pepper
- 2 bay leaves
- 1 tablespoon of salt
- 1 onion

Fluffy Egg Dressing:

- 4 hard boiled eggs
- 1 tablespoon of anchovy paste
- 3 tablespoons of chopped celery
- 1 teaspoon of Worcestershire sauce
- 1 teaspoon of dry mustard
- 1 ½ cups of chopped stuffed olives
- ¼ teaspoon of chopped garlic
- Tabasco sauce
- Salt to taste

DIRECTIONS:

Have redfish prepared as for baking. Remove head and tail. Wrap white string around the body of the fish to hold together and place fish, head, and tail in a large cooking vessel which has been filled ¾ full of water. Add seasoning and allow to come to a boil. Remove the head and tail almost as soon as the water begins to boil and place on a platter. Allow the body of the fish to boil for 25 minutes and lift carefully from the pot onto one side of the serving platter. Remove skin on the top side of the bone. Do not break the fish. Turn top half of the fish over to the center of the platter, lift out the back bone, and turn under side of the fish over on top of upper half, removing skin of second half. Place head and tail in position and chill. Decorate the fish from the neck to tail with 1 inch wide strips of finely chopped cooked beets, hard boiled egg yolks, and hard boiled egg whites. Alternate one row of red, white, and yellow. Place lemon slice in the mouth of the fish and garnish sides with lettuce leaves, sliced tomatoes, and sliced lemon. Serve with cold Fluffy Egg Dressing.

For Dressing: Mince eggs; add other ingredients and stir well. Use on cold fish platter. Serves 8.

TUNA TETRAZZINI
Mrs. Frances Gandy

INGREDIENTS:

- 2 cups of cooked macaroni
- 1 cup of water
- 3 tablespoons of butter
- ½ cup of cream
- 4 tablespoons of flour
- ½ cup of cheddar cheese
- ⅛ teaspoon of salt
- 2 cans of tuna
- 2 eggs
- 4 or 5 crackers

DIRECTIONS:

Place butter in a saucepan over low flame to melt, then add flour slowly until well blended. Add water slowly and stir mixture occasionally to prevent sticking to pan. Cook until thickened and remove from the flame. Add the cream and 2 well beaten eggs. Place a layer of macaroni in an oiled casserole dish, add a layer of tuna and next a layer of cheddar cheese (cut into slices 2 x 1 ½ x ⅛ inch thick). Pour about ½ of the sauce mixture over these ingredients and continue to add layers of macaroni, tuna, and cheese. Top with crushed cracker crumbs, dot with butter and sprinkle with paprika. Onion, garlic, or whole mushrooms may be added to this dish, if other seasoning is desirable. Mushroom soup may be substituted for the sauce, but eggs and cream should be included in the above proportions.

OYSTER AND CORN CASSEROLE
Mrs. Irene Edmonds (Tallahassee, FL)

INGREDIENTS:

- 2 small cans of whole kernel corn
- Milk
- Chives salt
- Celery salt
- 1 quart of oysters
- Salt and pepper
- 3 tablespoons of butter
- Buttered breadcrumbs
- 3 tablespoons of flour

DIRECTIONS:

Place oysters in a shallow skillet and heat until ends curl. Remove from fire. Melt butter in a saucepan and blend flour. Add oyster juice and enough milk to make 2 cups. Season with salt, pepper, celery salt, and chive salt to taste. Add oysters. Place some corn on the bottom of a buttered baking dish, then add a layer of the oyster mixture. Continue to alternate finishing with the oyster mixture. Cover with buttered crumbs; place in a 400 degree oven and allow to bake until crumbs are brown. Serve immediately.

RED BEAN CASSEROLE
Mrs. Tibbye Thomas

INGREDIENTS:

- 1 pound of ground beef
- 2 tablespoons of fat
- 2 ½ cups of red kidney beans, cooked
- 1 tablespoon of chili powder
- 2 cups of cooked tomatoes, drained
- ¼ cup green pepper, chopped
- 1 teaspoon of sugar
- 1 onion, chopped
- Pepper to taste
- 1 onion, chopped
- 1 bay leaf

Cornbread:

- ½ cup of cornmeal
- 1 teaspoon of paprika
- ½ cup of flour
- 1 egg
- 1 ½ teaspoons of baking powder
- ½ cup of milk
- ¼ teaspoon of salt
- 1 tablespoon of melted shortening
- Parsley, minced onion tops

DIRECTIONS:

Break ground beef into pieces and sauté in fat with onion and green pepper until the meat is browned. Season with salt, pepper, chili powder, and sugar. Add tomatoes, drained red beans, and bay leaf. Cover and simmer about 20 minutes. Remove bay leaf and place in a casserole dish.

To make the cornbread mixture: Sift dry ingredients into a bowl. Add egg, milk, shortening, and seasonings. Blend gently. Spoon over the casserole mixture and bake about 20 or 25 minutes at 400 degrees.

. . . .

DELUXE CAULIFLOWER CASSEROLE
Mrs. Lenora Cooper

INGREDIENTS:

- 1 large cauliflower or 2 frozen pkgs.
- 1 can of mushroom soup
- 4 tablespoons of parmesan cheese, grated
- ½ pound of small white onions, cooked
- ⅓ cup of milk
- 1 pound of shrimp, shelled and deveined
- 2 tablespoons of butter
- ⅛ teaspoon of black pepper

DIRECTIONS:

Heat oven to 375 degrees. Parbroil cauliflower. Break into medium size pieces. Add onions to cauliflower, drain cauliflower and onions well. Place in a greased two quart casserole dish. Dilute mushroom soup with milk. Add shrimp, butter, and pepper. Heat until butter melts. Pour mixture over cauliflower and onions. Sprinkle grated cheese on top. Bake covered for 20 minutes. Uncover, bake until golden brown. Serves 4.

TURKEY CASSEROLE
Mrs. Mary E. Slade

INGREDIENTS:

- 2 cups of noodles
- 2 cups of milk
- 1 pkg. of frozen broccoli
- 1 cup of grated processed American cheddar cheese
- 2 tablespoons of butter
- 2 tablespoons of flour
- 2 cups of diced cooked turkey (chicken or ham)
- 1 teaspoon of salt
- ¼ teaspoon of black pepper
- ¼ teaspoon of prepared mustard
- ⅓ cup of slivered blanched almonds, optional

DIRECTIONS:

Heat oven to 350 degrees. In a separate saucepan cook noodles and broccoli until tender in mildly salted water. Over low heat, melt butter in a saucepan and blend in flour. Add salt, pepper, mustard, and milk. Cook, stirring constantly, until mixture has thickened. Remove from heat and stir in cheese until melted. Drain noodles and broccoli. Dice broccoli stems. Leave flowerets whole. Arrange noodles, broccoli stems, and turkey in a shallow casserole dish. Pour cheese sauce over all. Loosen slightly to allow sauce to flow to bottom of dish. Arrange broccoli flowerets over top. Press slightly into sauce. Sprinkle with almonds. Bake until bubbling hot.

COMPANY CASSEROLE
Miss Ethel Mae Griggs

Place in a casserole dish, alternate layers of the following

- Cooked rice or spaghetti
- Sharp cheese, grated coarsely
- Slivers of baked or stewed chicken
- Rice or spaghetti
- Crab meat or lobster
- Cheese, season to taste
- 2 tablespoons of butter or margarine added to rice

Cover with cream of mushroom soup thinned with cream or milk. Cook in a moderate oven for 20 minutes at 350 degrees. Turkey may be substituted or added.

Vegetables

CELERY HEARTS WITH SPECIAL TOMATO SAUCE

Mrs. Mabel Armstrong (Wabasso, FL)

INGREDIENTS:

- 4 whole celery hearts
- 1 teaspoon of salt
- ¼ cup of water
- ¾ cup of catsup
- 1 tablespoon of vinegar
- 2 teaspoons of celery salt
- 3 garlic cloves
- 1 tablespoon of salad oil

DIRECTIONS:

Wash and tie a string around the celery hearts. Cook in boiling water for 15 or 20 minutes (until tender). Arrange cooked celery on a hot serving platter. Prepare sauce while celery is cooking. Prepare the sauce by rubbing a bowl generously with garlic. Leave ½ garlic clove in the bowl (stick toothpick with clove). Pour in catsup, salad oil, vinegar and celery salt. Mix well. Spoon sauce over each celery heart before serving.

CORN PUDDING

Mrs. Anne Teabeau

INGREDIENTS:

- 1 can of cream-style corn
- 1 ¼ teaspoons of salt
- 2 tablespoons of melted butter
- 1 cup of milk
- 2 tablespoons of flour
- 2 eggs, slightly beaten
- 1 tablespoon of sugar
- Pepper and mace
- Breadcrumbs
- Paprika

DIRECTIONS:

Combine corn, flour, sugar, and melted butter. Mix thoroughly, then add other ingredients. Sprinkle top lightly with bread or cracker crumbs and paprika. Bake in a buttered baking dish in a 325 degree oven until firm. Test as custard with a knife.

STUFFED EGGPLANT

Mrs. P. Q. Yancey (Atlanta, GA)

INGREDIENTS:

- ½ stick of butter
- 1 large eggplant
- ½ slice of ham (diced and fried)
- 1 medium onion, minced
- 1 garlic clove, peeled and finely chopped
- 2 tablespoons of chopped celery
- Breadcrumbs

DIRECTIONS:

Parboil eggplant. Cut eggplant in half, lengthwise, and scoop out pulp. Mash pulp and season to taste. Sauté the onion and celery in the heated butter. Add garlic, eggplant, and ham. Mix well. Fill eggplant shell with the mixture. Sprinkle the top with the breadcrumbs and dot with butter. Heat in a hot oven for about 10 minutes. Thyme, parsley, and pepper may be added for stronger seasoning.

 Cooked diced shrimp or American cheese can be substituted for the ham.

WEST INDIAN SCALLOPED POTATOES

Mrs. Lenora Cooper

INGREDIENTS:

- 4 cups of sliced, pared potatoes
- 1 teaspoon of pepper
- 2 large onions, minced
- 4 tablespoons of grated parmesan cheese
- 1 large bell pepper, minced
- ¼ pound of butter
- 1 can of mushroom soup
- 1 teaspoon of salt
- ⅓ cup of milk

DIRECTIONS:

Heat oven to 375 degrees. Mix onions, bell pepper, salt, and pepper. Arrange a layer of potatoes in a greased two quart casserole dish. Cover with a layer of onion and bell pepper mixture. Dot with butter. Repeat layers until ingredients are used up, ending with butter. Heat mushroom soup with milk and pour over ingredients in the casserole. Sprinkle grated cheese over the top. Bake covered for 45 minutes. Uncover, bake for 15 minutes longer or until golden brown and tender.

RICE – "ELEGANT VARIATIONS"
Coragreene Johnstone

- For four persons allow ⅔ cup of long grained rice, 4 cups of water, and 2 teaspoons of salt. Pick the rice to remove discolored kernels. Wash until the water is clear. Sprinkle the rice into the boiling water. Boil rapidly in an uncovered vessel until the grains are soft (usually not more than 20 minutes). Drain through a sieve; pour hot water through the rice to rinse off the starch; keep hot until serving time by placing the sieve over a vessel containing a small amount of boiling water.

LEMON RICE – Place a clove of garlic in the water used for steaming the rice. Sprinkle 1 teaspoon of lemon juice and 1 teaspoon of grated lemon rind over cooked rice and toss lightly. Good with fish.

OLIVE RICE – Toss ¼ cup of chopped stuffed olives and 2 teaspoons of melted butter with 3 cups of hot cooked rice.

PARSLEY RICE – Add ¼ cup of fresh parsley, coarsely chopped to 3 cups of cooked rice with ¼ cup of finely chopped onion sautéed in 3 tablespoons of butter. Good for chops and steaks.

ALMOND RICE – Sauté ¼ cup of slivered almonds in 2 tablespoons of butter until lightly toasted. Toss slightly with 3 cups of cooked rice and sprinkle liberally with paprika. Serve with chicken.

PEANUT RICE – Same as above only use peanuts.

SAFFRON RICE – Put a pinch of 3 stigmas added to the water in which the rice is cooked to give it a golden color and a slightly pungent flavor. Use with curry or other spicy dishes.

CHIVE RICE – 2 tablespoons of finely chopped chives added to 3 cups of cooked rice and 2 tablespoons of melted butter gives the dish an appetizing appearance and a mild onion flavor. Good with scrambled eggs or creamed dried beef.

RAISIN RICE – Simmer ¼ cup of seedless raisins in 2 cups of water until they are plump. Drain and toss lightly with 3 cups of cooked rice. Good with cubes of round steak that have been marinated in garlic flavored French dressing and broiled with onions and tomato wedges.

SPINACH SURPRISE
Ebony Test Kitchen

INGREDIENTS:

- 2 pounds of spinach
- 1 teaspoon of salt
- 2 medium onions
- ½ teaspoon of pepper
- 1 green pepper
- ½ teaspoon of garlic salt
- 3 tablespoons of butter or bacon fat
- ¼ cup of heavy cream
- 2 pimentos
- ¼ teaspoon of thyme

DIRECTIONS:

Wash and chop spinach fine. Sauté chopped onion, green pepper, and pimentos in butter. Add heavy cream and seasonings. Simmer for 10 minutes. Add spinach and continue to cook for 10 to 12 minutes, stirring frequently. Serve hot. Serves 4.

• •

SUCCOTASH
Mrs. Carmen Robinson

INGREDIENTS:

- ¼ pound ham
- 1 large onion
- 6 ears of corn
- 2 tomatoes, fresh or canned
- ½ bell pepper
- 1 pound of fresh Lima beans (or 1 pkg. frozen)
- 3 tablespoons of shortening
- Salt, pepper, and cayenne to taste

DIRECTIONS:

Cook Lima beans in a saucepan. Parbroil ham; cut into pieces and fry in shortening until nearly brown. Add chopped onion and pepper to ham and continue to fry to golden brown. Add tomatoes, cover and cook for 5 minutes. Cut corn from the cob, scraping off as much as possible. Add corn to the ham mixture and cook for 20 minutes, stirring occasionally. Add Lima beans and 1 ½ cups of water from beans to corn and ham. Simmer for ½ hour. Season to taste with pepper, cayenne, salt. Serves 6–8.

STEWED TOMATOES
Mrs. Charles S. Johnson (Nashville, TN)

INGREDIENTS:

- 12 ½ size can of tomatoes
- 2 tablespoons of brown sugar
- ¾ cup of rolled cracker crumbs
- 1 tablespoon of granulated sugar
- ½ teaspoon of salt
- ¼ stick of butter

DIRECTIONS:

Place in a quart sized saucepan the butter, cracker crumbs, and sugar. Heat until hot but not brown. Add tomatoes, stirring constantly. Allow to thicken over moderate heat, stirring frequently, pour into a buttered casserole dish and bake with a thin layer of rolled cornflakes topping.

SWEET AND SOUR GREEN BEANS
Mildred Hastings Swerdlow

INGREDIENTS:

- 1 pound of green beans
- 1 heaping tablespoon of schmaltz or butter
- ½ teaspoon of salt
- Pepper to taste
- 2 heaping tablespoons of brown sugar
- 1 bay leaf
- 2 tablespoons of vinegar
- 1 heaping teaspoon of whole cloves

DIRECTIONS:

Wash green beans and cut in desired lengths. Cover with water and bring to a boil. Add salt, pepper, bay leaf, and cloves. Reduce heat and cook at a slow boil until almost tender (about 20 minutes). Add schmaltz or butter, brown sugar, and vinegar. Continue cooking until beans are tender (about 10 minutes). Serves 6.

STUFFED MIRLITONS (Vegetable Pear)

Mae Colomb

INGREDIENTS:

- 6 vegetable pears (mirlitons)
- Dash of black pepper
- 1 pound of shrimp
    (chopped, peeled, and deveined)
- Dash of cayenne pepper
- 1 large onion
- Breadcrumbs
- 3 garlic cloves
- ¼ cup of chopped (fresh) parsley
- 1 bunch of shallots, minced
- 1 tablespoon of fat
- 1 sprig of thyme
- Salt to taste

DIRECTIONS:

Boil pears until tender, cut in half, remove seed, hull out meat, leave shells for stuffing. Peel and devein shrimp and chop very fine. Chop onions, shallots, and parsley. Place fat in frying pan, add onion and shallots. Simmer until soft. Add chopped shrimp, meat of pears, garlic, thyme, parsley, pepper, and salt. Cook until all water has been absorbed. Fill pear shells with the mixture. Sprinkle tops with breadcrumbs. Place in a 300 degree oven for 30 minutes.

Try waxing your ashtrays. Ashes won't cling, odors won't linger and then can be wiped clean with a paper towel or disposable tissue. This saves daily washing.

To remove burned food from oven, place small cloth saturated with ammonia in oven over night, and food can be easily wiped up.

Potatoes soaked in salt water for 20 minutes before baking will bake more rapidly.

For quick and handy seasoning while cooking, keep on hand a large shaker containing six parts of salt and one of pepper.

Bread crumbs added to scrambled eggs will improve the flavor and make larger helpings possible.

Sweet potatoes will not turn dark if put in salted water (5 teaspoons to 1 quart of water) immediately after peeling.

Soak bacon in cold water for a few minutes before placing in skillet. This will lessen the tendency to shrink and curl.

A tablespoon of vinegar added to the water when poaching eggs will help set the whites so they will not spread.

Wax the legs of your chairs and they will not mar the waxed floor when moved about.

Cut drinking straws into short lengths and insert through slits in pie crusts to prevent juice from running over in the oven and permit steam to escape.

Let raw potatoes stand in cold water for at least half an hour before frying to improve the crispness of french fried potatoes.

When cooking eggs it helps prevent cracking if you wet the shells in cold water before placing them in boiling water.

Breads, Rolls
Pies, and Pastry

BANANA BREAD

Mrs. Robert E. Jones (Waveland, MS)

INGREDIENTS:

- ¼ pound of butter or margarine
- 3 bananas
- 2 eggs
- 1 cup of sugar
- 1 teaspoon of soda
- 1 ½ cups of flour
- ¾ cup of broken pecans (optional)
- Salt

DIRECTIONS:

Cream butter, add sugar, then beaten eggs. Mash bananas, add soda, and stir. Add this to the first mixture. Add flour and salt. Beat well and pour into a greased loaf pan. Bake in a moderate oven for 350 degrees for about 45 minutes.

• •

CORN BREAD WITH A FUTURE

Ebony Test Kitchen

INGREDIENTS:

- ½ cup of chopped green onion tops
- 2 teaspoons of double acting baking powder
- 3 tablespoons of melted butter
- 1 cup of cornmeal
- ½ teaspoon of salt
- ½ cup of sifted flour
- 1 cup of undiluted Carnation evaporated milk
- 2 eggs

DIRECTIONS:

Sauté onion tops in butter. Do not brown. Sift dry ingredients into a bowl. Beat Carnation milk and eggs together with well sautéed onion tops and melted butter. Add to dry ingredients. Pour into buttered baking pan (8-inch square 1 ½ inches deep) or muffin tins. Bake in a moderate oven, 350 degrees for 20 to 30 minutes. In place of onions, try ½ cup of chopped celery leaves or coarsely grated American cheese.

CREAM PUFFS
Anita Gilbert

INGREDIENTS:

- 1 cup of water
- 5 tablespoons of butter or margarine
- 1 cup of flour
- 5 eggs
- Pinch of salt
- 1 teaspoon of baking powder
- 1 tablespoon of shortening
- Cream filling
- Whipped cream (optional)

DIRECTIONS:

Bring water, shortening, and salt to a rapid boil. Blend in flour until the mixture leaves the sides of the pan. Cool slightly. Beat in eggs, one at a time, then add baking powder. Beat for 150 strokes. Drop by tablespoonfuls into a greased muffin tin. Bake at 400 degrees for 20 minutes. Reduce heat and bake for 15 minutes longer. Cool, slit side, and remove excess dough. Fill with cream filling. Top with whipped cream if desired. Makes 18 puffs.

. . . .

OLD FASHIONED NUT LOAF
Mrs. Emilie Blanchard

INGREDIENTS:

- 2 cups of cake flour
- 1 cup of sugar
- 2 tablespoons of baking powder
- 3 eggs
- ½ teaspoon of salt
- 1 cup of nut meats, chopped
- ⅔ cup of butter
- 6 tablespoons of milk
- 1 teaspoon of vanilla

DIRECTIONS:

Sift flour, measure. Add baking powder and salt; sift together. Cream butter, add sugar gradually, and continue to cream until fluffy. Add eggs one at a time, beating after each addition. Add nuts; add flour alternately with milk. Beat well. Add vanilla. Bake in greased loaf pan in a 350 degree oven for 1 hour and 15 minutes.

PECAN PIE

Helen McClain (New Paltz, NY)

INGREDIENTS:

- 3 egg whites, beaten stiff

Add:

- 1 cup of granulated sugar
- ¾ cup of rolled graham crackers
- 1 ½ teaspoons of baking powder
- ¾ cup of chopped pecans
- 1 teaspoon of vanilla

DIRECTIONS:

Mix together, then put the mixture in a buttered 8-inch pie plate. Bake for 30 minutes at 300 degrees.

• •

GELATIN RUM CREAM PIE

Mrs. Verna Chambers (New York, NY)

INGREDIENTS:

- 6 egg yolks
- ½ cup of Jamaican rum
- ⅞ cup of sugar
- 1 pint of heavy cream
- 1 tablespoon of sugar
- ¼ cup of bitter sweet chocolate, grated
- ½ cup of cold water
- ¼ cup of pistachio nuts, finely shaved
- 1 gelatin package
- 1 pie shell

DIRECTIONS:

Mix together sugar, gelatin, and water in a sauce pan. Place over low heat and stir until gelatin is dissolved. Beat egg yolks and pour gelatin mixture slowly over eggs, beating constantly. When cold, stir in rum and fold in whipped cream. Pour into a baked pie shell. When set, sprinkle top with grated chocolate and shaved pistachio nuts.

Cakes, Cookies, and Icings

BANANA SPICE CAKE

Mrs. Edith Brooks (Los Angeles, CA)

INGREDIENTS:

- 2 cups of sifted flour
- 2 eggs
- ¾ cup of white sugar
- ¾ cup of milk
- 2 ½ teaspoons of baking powder
- 1 teaspoon of cinnamon
- 1 teaspoon of salt
- 1 teaspoon of allspice
- ½ cup of brown sugar
- ½ teaspoon of cloves
- ½ cup of margarine or Crisco
- 1 teaspoon of vanilla

Banana Icing:

- 1 large ripe banana, mashed
- 2 cups of powdered sugar
- ½ teaspoon of lemon juice
- 2 drops of yellow food coloring
- 2 teaspoons of creamed butter
- ½ pint of whipped cream

DIRECTIONS:

Cream margarine and brown sugar. Add ½ cup of milk, beat well. Add eggs. Sift together dry ingredients; add margarine mixture alternately with ¼ cup of milk. Add vanilla and beat for 2 minutes. Pour into a greased ring pan well lined with waxed paper. Bake at 350 degrees for 40 minutes. Allow to cool before turning out of pan. Ice with Banana Icing. Before serving fill center with whipped cream into which a pinch of grated lemon peel and finely chopped banana have been folded.

For Icing: Blend sifted powdered sugar with creamed butter alternately with mashed banana and lemon juice. Add food coloring, blend well and spread on cake.

BLACKBERRY JAM CAKE
Mrs. Mildred Crawford

INGREDIENTS:

- 1 cup of butter
- ½ teaspoon of allspice
- 1 cup of sugar
- ½ teaspoon of cinnamon or nutmeg
- 3 egg yolks
- ½ cup of sour milk
- 2 cups of flour
- 1 cup of blackberry jam
- 1 teaspoon of soda
- 1 teaspoon of vanilla
- 3 egg whites

Icing:

- 2 cups of sugar
- 1 cup of milk
- ½ stick of butter

DIRECTIONS:

Sift dry ingredients into a bowl. Add butter, egg yolks, sour milk, then beat with an electric mixer at a low speed for 2 minutes or 200 strokes by hand. Add vanilla and blackberry jam. Beat for 1 minute or until well mixed. Bake in two 8-inch layer pans for 20–25 minutes at 375 degrees.

For Icing: Place ingredients in a saucepan, boil until a soft ball forms in cold water. Let cool, then whip and spread on layers.

BLACK CHOCOLATE CAKE
Mrs. Hertha Taylor

INGREDIENTS:

- 2 cups of flour
- 1 cup of thick sour cream
- 1 ½ cups of sugar
- 1 cup of hot water or coffee
- 1 cup of shortening
- 1 teaspoon of soda
- 2 eggs, separated
- 2 squares of chocolate

DIRECTIONS:

Cream shortening, add sugar, beat in egg yolks, and blend. Add alternately flour and sour cream. Add hot liquid to which grated chocolate and soda have been added. Fold in stiffly beaten egg whites. Pour into a greased baking pan and bake in a slow oven, 325 degrees. Frost if desired.

PINEAPPLE UPSIDE DOWN CAKE

Mrs. Willis J. King

INGREDIENTS:

- ½ cup of butter or margarine
- 2 cups of light brown sugar
- 2 cups of diced canned pineapples
- ½ cup of pecans, shelled

DIRECTIONS:

Melt butter and sugar in a heavy skillet. Remove from the fire, cover with pineapple and pecans. Top with plain cake mix or your favorite cake batter. Bake in 350 degree oven for 20–25 minutes. Serve hot or cold with whipped cream if desired.

• •

BUTTER COOKIES

Mrs. Adam Ratliff

INGREDIENTS:

- ½ pound of butter
- 1 egg
- 1 cup of sugar
- 3 cups of flour
- 1 teaspoon of vanilla

DIRECTIONS:

Cream butter and sugar until all sugar has dissolved. Add egg and mix for about 5 minutes. Add vanilla. Add 1 cup of flour with the mixer, add remaining 2 cups of flour with a spoon. Fill Ateco cookie machine with dough and run out different design cookies on an ungreased cookie pan. Bake at 350 degrees for about 20 minutes.

BUTTER COOKIES SUPREME

Miss Vera Jenkins

INGREDIENTS:

- ½ pound of butter
- 1 ¼ teaspoons of baking powder
- 3 cups of flour
- 2 teaspoons of vanilla
- 1 ½ cups of sugar
- 1 egg
- 2 teaspoons of whipped cream

DIRECTIONS:

Sift all dry ingredients, then blend in butter. Beat egg, cream, and vanilla together; add to dry mixture, blend thoroughly. Roll out on floured board and cut. Bake in a 400 degree oven. For interesting variations, add ½ cup of raisins or currants or chopped peanuts or walnut meats.

· ·

BUTTERSCOTCH SLICES

Mrs. Alice Tull (Jefferson City, MO)

INGREDIENTS:

- 2 cups of sifted flour
- ½ teaspoon of baking soda
- ¾ cup of shortening
- ½ teaspoon of cream of tartar
- 1 cup of brown sugar, packed
- ½ teaspoon of salt
- 1 cup of milk
- ½ teaspoon of vanilla
- 1 egg
- ½ cup of finely chopped walnuts or pecans

DIRECTIONS:

Cream shortening, brown sugar; add egg, beat until creamy. Sift dry ingredients and add to creamed mixture. Add vanilla and nuts and blend well. Shape dough into a roll about 2 inches in diameter. Wrap and chill for several hours in the refrigerator. Slice dough ⅛ inch thick. Place on an ungreased cookie sheet and bake in a 375 degree oven for 8 to 10 minutes. Yields 4 to 5 dozen cookies.

CINNAMON REFRIGERATOR COOKIES

Mrs. Gertrude Holmes

INGREDIENTS:

- 3 ½ cups of sifted flour
- 1 teaspoon of baking soda
- 1 cup of shortening
- 1 tablespoon of cinnamon
- 1 cup of brown sugar
- ¼ teaspoon of salt
- 1 cup of white sugar
- 1 cup of very finely chopped nuts
- 2 eggs

DIRECTIONS:

Sift flour, soda, cinnamon, salt together. Cream shortening until light and soft. Add both brown and white sugar gradually, creaming constantly. Beat eggs until light, stir into creamed mixture. Stir in sifted dry ingredients, about a cupful at a time. Add nuts. When batter is thoroughly mixed, divide dough in halves or thirds and roll each into a long roll on a sheet of waxed paper. Wrap and store in the refrigerator overnight. Slice cookies very thin and bake on greased baking sheet until light brown. Makes 8 dozen.

· ·

DATE AND NUT CHEWS

Mrs. Edith Brooks (Los Angeles, CA)

INGREDIENTS:

- 2 eggs
- ¼ teaspoon of salt
- 1 cup of sugar
- 1 cup of dates (pitted and chopped)
- ¾ cup of flour
- 1 cup of chopped pecans or English walnuts
- 1 teaspoon of baking powder

DIRECTIONS:

Beat eggs, add sugar; beat until well blended. Mix ¼ cup of flour with chopped dates and nuts. Sift remaining flour with baking powder and salt. Add to egg mixture and beat until all ingredients are well blended. Pour batter into a well greased shallow pan. Spread thinly. Bake in a moderate oven at 350 degrees for 30 minutes; cool; cut into bars with a sharp knife.

MACAROONS
Mrs. Amelia Linton

INGREDIENTS:

- 3 egg whites
- 3 cups of ground pecans
- ½ box of light brown sugar
- 2 teaspoons of vanilla
- Dash of salt

DIRECTIONS:

Beat egg whites until stiff, add brown sugar, pecans, and vanilla. Drop mixture by spoonfuls on a greased cookie sheet. Bake for 1 hour in a slow oven.

AUNT AMY'S COOKIES
Miss Virginia Cates

INGREDIENTS:

- 1 cup of flour
- ½ cup of white sugar
- ½ teaspoon of soda
- 1 cup of brown sugar, or light
- ¼ teaspoon of baking powder
- ½ teaspoon of salt
- 1 egg
- ½ teaspoon of cinnamon, if desired
- 1 teaspoon of vanilla
- 1 cup of grape nut flakes
- ½ cup of shortening
- 1 cup of quick cooking oats

DIRECTIONS:

Sift flour with soda, baking powder, salt, and cinnamon. Cream shortening (use vegetable fat or part butter or margarine) and cream sugars until light and fluffy. Add flour and remaining ingredients. Arrange by teaspoonfuls on a buttered cookie sheet. Flatten with a knife dipped in water. For very delicate cookies, flatten until the cookies are almost paper thin, a slow task but a rewarding one. Bake in a moderate oven at 350 degrees for 8 to 10 minutes or until delicately brown. Remove from cookie sheet while still warm. Makes 60.

DELICIOUS ICE CREAM

Margaret Davis Bowen (Atlanta, GA)

INGREDIENTS:

- ½ pint of cream
- 2 eggs, separated
- 1 can (46 ounces) of pineapples or apricot juice
- 1 cup of sugar
- 3 or 4 crushed bananas or crushed peaches

DIRECTIONS:

Whip a ½ pint of heavy cream, and whites of two eggs, beaten stiff. Stir in whipped cream. Add fruit. Flavor with almond or vanilla extract and the juice of a small lemon. Use almond extract when crushed peaches are used.

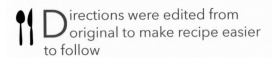

Directions were edited from original to make recipe easier to follow

COFFEE ICE CREAM

Mrs. Emma Brown

INGREDIENTS:

- ⅔ cup of canned sweetened condensed milk
- ¾ cup of strong black coffee
- 1 teaspoon of vanilla extract
- ⅛ teaspoon of salt
- 1 cup of light or heavy cream, whipped

DIRECTIONS:

Combine milk, coffee, salt, and vanilla. Then chill. Whip cream, fold into chilled mixture. Turn into freezing tray of refrigerator and freeze until frozen with control at coldest setting. Turn into a bowl and beat well with an egg beater, then return to freezing tray and freeze until firm.

PEARL'S SPECIAL DESSERT

Mrs. Pearl Gore (Tallahassee, FL)

Purchase from bakery a large orange chiffon cake with a hole in center. Fill center hole with fruit Jello (black raspberry, cherry, or mixed flavors for color) and fruit cocktail.

Whip 2 small cartons of whipping cream, flavor with rum flavoring, sugar to taste and ice cake. Jello may be added around edges and sprinkled in spots over the cake for looks.

DATE SOUFFLE
Mrs. Harriet Holmes

INGREDIENTS:

- 2 tablespoons of butter
- 3 egg yolks
- 3 tablespoons of sugar
- 3 egg whites
- 2 tablespoons of flour
- 1 pkg. dates, chopped
- 1 pinch of salt
- ¼ cup of milk

Orange Sauce:

- 1 cup of sugar
- 1 tablespoon of cornstarch
- 1 cup of orange juice
- 1 tablespoon of butter
- 1 egg yolk
- 1 juice of a lemon
- 1 orange rind, grated

DIRECTIONS:

Cream together butter and sugar. Add egg yolks, flour, and milk. Beat well. Add chopped dates, and fold in egg whites stiffly beaten with salt. Place in greased baking dish; place dish in a pan of water. Bake in 350 degree oven for 35 minutes. Serve with orange sauce.

For Orange Sauce: Mix together all ingredients and cook in a double boiler until mixture coats the spoon.

• •

MRS. TRUNDY'S INDIAN PUDDING
Mrs. Walter P. Colteryahn (Pittsburgh, PA)

INGREDIENTS:

- 3 tablespoons of cornmeal
- 2 tablespoons of brown sugar
- 3 tablespoons of minute tapioca
- 2 beaten eggs
- 1 teaspoon of salt
- ½ teaspoon of cinnamon
- 1 quart of milk
- ½ teaspoon of ginger
- 3 tablespoons of molasses
- ¼ teaspoon of nutmeg

DIRECTIONS:

Add 1 pint of milk to cornmeal, tapioca, and salt. Cook in a double boiler till thick. Add remaining ingredients and remainder of milk. Stir. Pour into buttered casserole dish. Bake at 350 degrees for 1 hour.

LEMON DELIGHT

Mrs. Julia Duncan

INGREDIENTS:

- 4 eggs
- 1 cup of sugar
- Rind of 2 lemons
- 1 pint of milk
- ¾ cup of graham crackers
- 3 tablespoons of Knox gelatin
- Juice of 3 lemons

DIRECTIONS:

Separate eggs. Beat yolks until light. Add sugar. Heat milk to a boiling point; add to egg and sugar mixture. Add gelatin which has been softened in lemon juice; add rind. Fold entire mixture into stiffly beaten egg whites. Pour into a pan that has been greased with butter and lined with crushed graham crackers to form a crust. Put into a refrigerator to set. Top with whipped cream. A spring or mold pan should be used.

. . . .

CAKE TOP LEMON PUDDING Prize winning recipe – second prize.

Mrs. Juliet Walker-Mitchell

INGREDIENTS:

- 2 tablespoons of butter or margarine
- ½ cup of lemon juice
- 1 ½ cups of sugar
- 3 eggs
- ¼ teaspoon of salt
- 1 ¼ cups of undiluted evaporated milk
- ⅓ cup of flour

DIRECTIONS:

Mix together softened butter and sugar. Add flour, salt, and lemon juice. Separate eggs. Mix beaten yolks with milk and add mixture. Beat stiffly the whites of eggs and fold into the custard. Pour into a baking dish. Set dish in a pan of water. Bake for 45 minutes in a moderate oven at 325 degrees. When done there will be a lemon custard at bottom and lemon cake at the top.

MOCHA SOUFFLE
Mrs. Harriet Holmes

INGREDIENTS:

- 2 egg yolks
- ¼ cup of sugar
- 4 egg whites
- ½ cup of flour
- ½ cup of hot milk
- ½ cup of strong coffee

Brandy Sauce:

- 3 tablespoons of butter
- ½ cup of powdered sugar
- 1 tablespoon of cognac
- 2 egg yolks
- ½ cup of cream
- 1 pinch of salt

DIRECTIONS:

Beat the egg yolks until light, add gradually sugar, salt, and flour mixed together. Add the mixture to coffee and hot milk. Beat egg whites until stiff, fold in. Bake for 35 minutes in a greased mold (400 degree oven). Serve with brandy sauce.

For Sauce: Cream butter, gradually add powdered sugar. Drop by drop stir in cognac. Beat in egg yolks, salt, and cream. Cook in a double boiler until thick. Serve hot.

• •

DELICIOUS OLD-FASHIONED BREAD PUDDING
Estelle Turpin

INGREDIENTS:

- 6 slices of stale bread
- ½ cup of butter
- 2 eggs
- 1 cup of sugar
- 2 cups of milk
- 1 cup of raisins
- Dash of cinnamon (powder)
- ½ cup of heavy cream or evaporated milk
- 2 teaspoons of vanilla
- 2 cups of whipped egg whites

DIRECTIONS:

Mix eggs, butter, milk, cream, and sugar well. Add bread that has been dampened with milk. Sprinkle cinnamon and nutmeg into mixture. Add vanilla and raisins. Pour into baking dish and place in an oven at 350 degrees for 40 minutes. Remove and cover top with ½-inch layer of jelly and over this, spread stiffly whipped sweetened egg whites. Place in an oven again until the top is golden brown.

DILLARD AUXILIARY'S INTERNATIONAL FOOD FESTIVAL COOKBOOK:
PRESIDENT SAMUEL DUBOIS COOK, 1973–1997
"THE DILLARD UNIVERSITY EXPERIENCE IS GLOBAL"

A college or university ought to be one of the most exciting places in society. Although the essence of the academy is the "community of scholars," that community does not exhaust the meaning, vitality, and variety of experiences on the campus. Extracurricular and co-curricular activities enhance and enrich the academic enterprise for all constituents—students, faculty, staff, administrators, trustees, and friends.

Dillard is a very special place. It is a place of excitement, meaning, dynamic interactions, creative encounters, and joy. It harbors and begets the richness of diversity, individuality, and the common life. Beyond the challenge and joys of the strictly academic enterprise are numerous other activities: intercollegiate and intramural sports, art exhibits, plays, student publications, all kinds of musical entertainment, a multiplicity of religious experiences, fraternities, sororities, and other social organizations, a long list of rewarding activities offered by residential life, picnics, cookouts, informal games, and so forth. There is no reason to be bored at Dillard.

This Cookbook, carefully compiled and edited by Jacqueline G. Houston and Dr. Keith M. Wismar, is a superb and indeed classic example of the richness and vitality of diversity of the Dillard experience. The International Food Festival, like the Dillard Auxiliary, has become an institution on this campus. It helps to make the Dillard experience inclusive, total, rich, and unique.

This Cookbook contains the recipes of exotic cuisine and dishes from around the world: African, Creole, Oriental, Cajun, "Soul," French, Southwestern United States, German, Spanish, Caribbean, South American, etc. All kinds of succulent specialties are included. What a treat, challenge, and opportunity.

Portrait of students outside of school building, 1977

Cooking is a great art. And a great "fine art" at that. To learn and master delicate new recipes is a special artistic experience and source of enjoyment and expanded self-esteem and self-confidence.

The Dillard Auxiliary, of which Dr. Houston is President, is to be commended. And so is the International Food Festival, under the magnificent direction of Dr. Elton C. Harrison, Vice President for Academic Affairs and Vice President for Administration and Planning.

Above all, I want to commend Dr. Houston and Dr. Wismar on their tireless efforts in the conceptualization, design, completion, and publication of this wonderful and exciting Cookbook. This Cookbook should and will bring a lot of pleasure and enjoyment to a lot of people. It also adds to the long and distinguished list of cookbooks published in New Orleans. Dillard does it again!

Samuel Duboois Cook
President, Dillard University

From the *Dillard Auxiliary's International Food Festival Cookbook*

DILLARD AUXILIARY'S

International Food Festival
COOKBOOK

Premier Edition

CORNED BEEF STEW

Mr. Christian Fugar
Division of Business

INGREDIENTS:

- 2 pounds of tomatoes
- ½ teaspoon of red pepper
- Cooking oil
- Corned beef
- ½ chopped onion
- Eggs (boiled)

DIRECTIONS:

Put oil in a pan and mix with onions and peppers. Let fry for about 7 minutes, add corned beef and let fry for another 7 minutes. Boil eggs, slice them, and place them on the stew.

FRIED PLANTAIN

Mr. Christian Fugar
Division of Business

INGREDIENTS:

- Plantain
- Cooking oil
- Powdered sugar

DIRECTIONS:

Fry sliced plantain in cooking oil until brown. Remove, drain excess oil, and sprinkle with powdered sugar (optional).

FRIED YAMS

Mr. Christian Fugar
Division of Business

INGREDIENTS:

- African White Yams
- 6 eggs
- Cooking oil

DIRECTIONS:

Boil yams, then remove from water and fry in eggs until golden brown. Remove, strain, and serve.

GROUND NUT STEW

A traditional West African Stew with or without meat.

Dr. Shelby Faye Lewis
Division of Social Sciences

INGREDIENTS:

- 1 cup of chopped onions
- 1 cup of chopped celery
- 1 cup of chopped green peppers
- ¼ cup of flour
- ⅛ cup of vegetable oil
- 4 cups of chopped tomatoes
- 3 cups of water
- 1 cup of roasted ground peanuts
- 10 pounds of skinned chicken
- Chili peppers
- Season to taste

DIRECTIONS:

Brown flour in oil. In a separate pan, sauté chopped seasonings. Blend flour and sauté vegetables together and add water. Add tomatoes, season with salt, pepper, chili peppers. Add peanuts. Add boiled skinned chicken pieces. Simmer for ½ hour. Serve over cooked rice with condiments (raisins, chopped bananas, apples, cucumbers, etc.).

• •

MOI MOI

Azubike Okpalaeze
Data Processing Center

INGREDIENTS:

- Black eye peas, ground up
- Spices, season to taste
- Ground beef
- Boiled eggs, sliced

DIRECTIONS:

Mix peas and spices. Add ground beef (un-cooked). Slice eggs and place in the center of a cup and cover with aluminum foil. Bake at 350 degrees for 1 ½ hours.

JOLLOF RICE

Traditionally prepared to make a girl or boy fall in love with you.

Dr. Anthony Osei
Division of Business

INGREDIENTS:

- Corned beef
- 2 ½ pounds of tomatoes
- 1 cup mixed vegetables
- 1 cup cooking oil
- ½ cup chopped onions
- Dash of pepper
- Dash of salt
- Rice

DIRECTIONS:

In a large skillet, place oil and brown onions. Add a dash of pepper, and then add tomatoes. Add vegetables and mashed corned beef. Wash rice and add to mixture. Add ½ cup of water, a dash of salt, and let cook for 25–30 minutes.

· ·

SPINACH STEW

Dr. Anthony Osei
Division of Business

INGREDIENTS:

- About 1 ½ pounds chopped spinach
- ½ cup chopped onions
- 1 pound tomatoes
- 1 teaspoon of pepper oil
- 1 ½ teaspoons of salt
- 2 pounds of mackerel fish (canned)

DIRECTIONS:

In skillet, let oil get hot and add onions. Sauté onions until light brown. Add pepper, tomatoes, and let cook for about 15 minutes. Add spinach and let cook for five minutes. Add canned fish and cook on a low flame for about 10 minutes.

CLAM DIP

Dr. Winona Somervill
Division of Social Sciences

INGREDIENTS:

- 2 packages of cream cheese
- 2 cans of Gordon minced clams
- 1 large garlic, minced
- ½ teaspoon of Worcestershire sauce
- ¼ teaspoon of salt
- ¼ teaspoon of Tabasco sauce
- ⅛ teaspoon of red pepper

DIRECTIONS:

Thin cheese with ¼ cup of sour cream. Mix in remaining ingredients, chill, and serve.

· ·

GREEN BEAN CASSEROLE (TEXAS STYLE)

Dr. Bennie Webster
Division of Education

INGREDIENTS:

- 2 cans of French style cut green beans
- 1 can of cream of mushroom soup
- 1 can of refried onions
- ⅔ cup of milk
- Season with black pepper

DIRECTIONS:

Strain 2 cans cut green beans and add 1 can cream of mushroom soup, along with ⅔ cup of milk. Mix in refried dried onions. Stir in pepper (season to taste). Let mixture bake for about 30 to 35 minutes. Save small amount of onions and cover top of casserole with them. Bake for an additional 5 minutes. Let cool and serve.

Green Bean Casserole is prepared for about 6 servings. A very good vegetable dish to serve for dinner with broiled or baked chicken and a noodle dish on the side. Dish is low in calories.

FRIED EGG ROLL

Mrs. Marivic D. Ortiz-Luis
Office of the Registrar

INGREDIENTS:

- 1 pound of ground pork
- ¼ pound of shrimp, shell out, deveined, and chopped
- ½ cup of chopped carrots
- ½ cup of chopped water chestnuts
- ¼ cup chopped green onions
- 1 teaspoon of salt
- ½ teaspoon of pepper
- 1 egg
- 25 egg roll wrappers

DIRECTIONS:

Mix well all the ingredients. Cut the wrapper into half. Spoon the mixture into the wrapper and wrap. Deep fry egg rolls.

 Serve as an appetizer and dip in sweet and sour sauce. This is an oriental dish from the Philippines.

CHINESE CHICKEN (TENO STYLE)

Mrs. Elois Teno
Secretary, Office of Development

INGREDIENTS:

- 2 medium size spring chickens
- 8 ounces LaChoy Soy Sauce
- 1 cup of honey
- 1 cup of water
- 1 whole shallot (green onions)
- 4 sliced mushrooms

DIRECTIONS:

In a large sauce pan, using enough water to cover the chicken, boil cut up chicken ½ hour on each side. Add honey and simmer until mixture becomes thick. Cut up and add shallots and mushrooms. Put chicken in a broiler and pour liquid over to glaze it. Chicken has to be served with rice. Liquid mixture can be put on rice as desired.

GRILLADES

Mrs. Marie Wiggan Houston
(Dr. Houston's mother)

INGREDIENTS:

- 10 seven steaks
- 1 whole head garlic
- 1 cup of flour
- 1 cup of cooking oil
- Season-All
- Cayenne pepper

DIRECTIONS:

Put half cooking oil in a large heavy pot. Season meat to taste with Season-All and cayenne pepper on both sides. Leave drippings in pot and add oil as you need to keep from sticking. Your drippings are continuously browning, don't worry, they will make a beautiful gravy. Peel garlic and chop real fine while browning steaks. When you finish browning, you should have used up all of the cooking oil. Put flour into this until it has absorbed all of the oil. Put garlic in and mix up real well. Place meat back in pot and cover with water. Let simmer on low fire until tender, about 2 hours. Now you have a delicious dish that can be served best over steamed rice or grits.

CRAWFISH BISQUE

Ms. Karen Lawrence Pleas
Clerical Assistant, Title III Office

INGREDIENTS:

- 5 pounds crawfish meat
- 7 pounds of crawfish (scalded and cleaned for just the heads)
- 1 large onion
- 1 ½ cups of parsley
- 1 bell pepper
- 1 tablespoon of garlic salt
- 1 cap full of Worcestershire sauce
- 2 cups of stale breadcrumbs
- 2 (8-ounce) cans of tomato paste

DIRECTIONS:

Clean crawfish heads thoroughly and set aside. Mix crawfish meat and stale breadcrumbs along with onions, bell pepper, parsley. Season with garlic salt, Worcestershire sauce. In a large skillet cook mixture until brown, adding heads. Make a red gravy using tomato paste. In just a little cooking oil brown ¼ of (chopped) onions, bell pepper, and tomato paste. Add about 4 (8-ounce) cans of water and a dash of parsley. Bring to a boil, turn flame to medium, and let simmer for 10 minutes until slightly thicker. Add heads and simmer for about 20 minutes. Then you have a rare treat. Best when served over rice.

This is a quaint old Creole recipe handed down from generation to generation. It is quite popular with native New Orleanians and a rare treat for any seafood lover.

JAMBALAYA

Mrs. Dorothy S. Randolph
Dillard Auxiliary Supporter

INGREDIENTS:

- 10 cups of long grain rice for 10 cups of liquid
- 3 pounds of shrimp, deveined
- 2–3 pounds of crawfish meat
- ½ cup of diced fresh pork
- 1 cup of diced fresh veal
- 2 cups of diced ham
- 3 cups of diced smoked sausage
- 1 cup of diced hot sausage
- 4 cups of chopped onions
- 3 cups of chopped green peppers
- 2 cups of chopped garlic
- 4 cups of chopped celery
- 2 cups of chopped parsley
- 1 teaspoon of thyme
- 1 tablespoon of basil
- 5 bay leaves (approximately)
- 4 cups of chopped tomatoes (canned or fresh)

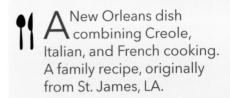

A New Orleans dish combining Creole, Italian, and French cooking. A family recipe, originally from St. James, LA.

DIRECTIONS:

Prepare stock. Before heading shrimp, wash thoroughly. Head shrimp and boil heads until the water is reduced to approximately 3–4 cups. Boil beef soup meat (bones and meat) and ham bones with onions, garlic until stock is reduced to approximately 3–4 cups. Steam lightly salted chicken until tender enough to bone easily. Put chicken meat aside, boil chicken parts until chicken stock is reduced to 3–4 cups. Drain tomatoes. Keep liquid and discard all solids from stock and mix all liquids 10–12 cups. In a heavy pot, slowly fry all seasonings—onions, garlic, etc. until onions are transparent. Stir frequently but keep pot frying at all times. Add tomatoes to fry, add pork to fry, add veal to fry, add sausage—hot and smoked to fry, add ham, chicken, crawfish, and shrimp, add ⅓ cup of stock. Keep at a rapid boil. Add washed long grain rice. Stir well while cooking briskly. Add salt, black pepper, and hot pepper to taste. Let pot simmer over low flame. After 5 minutes—stir well. After 10 minutes—stir well. Keep covered and cook over low flame until rice is cooked. During cooking time, lift ingredients from pan bottom with spatula, do not stir again.

Tip: Tomatoes must be fried till cooked. Fresh tomatoes must be fried longer than canned tomatoes.

CATFISH FINGERS IN GARLIC SAUCE

This is a "to taste" dish. (I like it "hot" and garlicky)

Patricia Saul Rochon
Coordinator, Mass Communications
Division of Humanities

INGREDIENTS:

- Cat fish fingers
- Lemon juice
- Tony Chachere's seasonings
- Garlic, fresh and crushed
- Butter

DIRECTIONS:

Sauté garlic in butter. Add lemon juice. Sprinkle Chachere's seasoning over catfish fingers and sauté in lemon, butter, garlic sauce. Dish is ready when fish flakes easily with fork. Alternatively, fish or fillets can be seasoned placed in a pan and the sauce poured over them. If you have a crowd, they can be layered and baked in the oven at 325 degrees.

NEW ORLEANS FRENCH MARKET BEAN SOUP

Adapted from a recipe in a Picayune (Mississippi) newspaper.

Dr. Jeffery Smith
Division of Natural Sciences

INGREDIENTS:

- 2 pounds of canned tomatoes, drained and chopped
- 1 green pepper, diced
- 2 medium onions, chopped
- 6 stalks of celery, with leaves, chopped
- 2 cloves garlic, chopped
- 1 pound smoked sausage, sliced
- 4 chicken breasts
- 1 ham steak (or ham for seasoning)
- 2 tablespoons of Creole seasoning
- ⅓ cup of each of the following dried beans:
    baby white limas
    barley
    black beans (or turtle beans)
    black eye peas
    chick peas (garbanzos)
    green peas
    lentils
    navy beans
    pinto beans
    red beans

DIRECTIONS:

Wash bean mix and add water to cover. Add 1 tablespoon of salt and soak overnight. Drain, add 3 quarts water and 1 ham steak (or ham for seasoning) and let simmer for 3 hours or until beans are tender. Add the tomatoes, pepper, onions, celery, and garlic and season to taste. Simmer for 90 minutes, uncovered, add smoked sausage and chicken breasts. Then add Creole seasoning and let simmer until chicken is tender. Remove chicken, debone, chop, and return to pot. Simmer until ready to serve.

 2 packages of frozen seasoning mix may be substituted for the onions, green pepper, and celery.

JUDE'S BOILED CRAWFISH

Dr. Jude Sorapuru
Chairperson, Division of Education

INGREDIENTS:

- 40–50 pounds of live crawfish (1 sack)
- 2 boxes of table salt
- 2 (8-ounce) bottles of cayenne pepper
- 1 stalk of celery
- 2 fluid ounces of liquid crab boil
- 6 packages of dry crab boil mix
- 1 dozen lemons sliced and squeezed
- 3 pounds of onions cut in half
- 2 pounds of potatoes and 6 ears of corn

"This Boiled Crawfish recipe originated in the wilds of St. John Parish and is a Sorapuru Family Tradition."

DIRECTIONS:

To a large (40 qt.) pot ½ full of water add all of the above ingredients, except the crawfish. Bring water and seasonings to a full boil and cook for 15–20 minutes to distribute seasoning. While waiting for water to boil wash crawfish twice and remove any dead ones. After seasoning mix has boiled for 15 to 20 minutes, add the crawfish (which will cause boil to stop). When the water begins to boil again, the crawfish are done. Turn off the heat and let the crawfish soak in the seasoned water for 20–25 minutes. Drain crawfish and serve piping hot on newspaper with ice cold beer and soft drinks. The boiled potatoes, onions, and corn may be served as a side dish.

STUFFED PEPPERS WITH SHRIMP

Mrs. Evelyn Wismar
(Dr. Keith Wismar's Mother)

INGREDIENTS:

- 6 whole fresh bell peppers
  (sliced in half, cleaned, and drained)
- 2–3 pounds of fresh shrimp
- 3 whole yellow onions
  (diced medium size)
- 2–3 cups of French breadcrumbs
- 1 stick of real butter
- Salt, pepper, and garlic powder or cloves

"Stuffed Peppers with Shrimp has been a Wismar family favorite for several generations. It has its origins in the Creole cooking history of New Orleans and highlights the holy three of New Orleans cookery: onions, sweet pepper, and garlic."

DIRECTIONS:

Peel and devein shrimp. Chop into medium pieces and put aside in colander to drain. Peel and chop onions, then brown onions in 1 tablespoon of butter and put aside. Brown shrimp in 2 tablespoons of butter until most of the liquid is reduced. Add browned onions to shrimp and add rest of butter. Season with salt and pepper to taste. Add garlic powder or fresh garlic to taste. Add 2–3 cups of breadcrumbs until it makes a thick stuffing. You may add 1 tablespoon of milk if necessary. Check seasoning to taste. Stuff sweet pepper halves with dressing. Sprinkle top with dressing. Bake in 350 degree oven for 45 minutes. Makes twelve peppers.

TEXAS CHILI

Mr. W. Timothy Beckett
(Helen Beckett's Husband)

INGREDIENTS:

- 2 large onions
- 3 garlic cloves
- 2 ½ pounds of ground beef
- 3 ounces of Mexene Chili Powder

DIRECTIONS:

Put 2 ½ tablespoons of oil to coat bottom of a pan. Sauté onions and garlic on a low flame. When glazed add 2 ½ pounds of ground beef, stir continuously until brown. Add one cup of water and keep stirring (don't let mixture stick). Add another cup of water. When this cooks down, meat should be done. Add 3 ounces of Mexene Chili Powder and stir. When this cooks down, add water to cover. If beans are added use ranch style. The secret of this chili is Mexene Chili Powder.

• •

IT'S NOT EXACTLY MACARONI AND CHEESE

Dr. Allan Burkett
Division of Natural Sciences

INGREDIENTS:

- 2 tablespoons of flour
- 2 tablespoons of butter
- 2 cups of elbow macaroni, uncooked
- ¼ cup of minced onion
- 2 cups of milk
- 12 ounces of sharp cheese (grated)
- ½ cup of salad olives
- 1 can of corned beef

DIRECTIONS:

Hydrolize the pasta (i.e. cook the stuff). Melt butter in a saucepan, add flour to prepare roux, and slowly add milk with stirring. Bring to a boil. Add dried onion and continue heating until sauce begins to thicken. Add cheese and remove from heat. Stir until cheese melts. Place cooked macaroni, corned beef, olives, and cheese sauce in a casserole dish. Bake at 350 degrees for 30 minutes or on high in a microwave for 8–10 minutes.

MONIQUE'S CHILI
This spicy dish originated in Port Sulfur, LA

Monica D. Courvertier
(Dr. Patricia Morris' Sister)

INGREDIENTS:

- ¾ cup of chili powder
- 3 large bell peppers, chopped
- 2 tablespoons of cayenne pepper
- 3 large onions, chopped
- 2 garlic heads, chopped
- 2 pounds of ground chuck, cooked and drained
- 12 ounces Big R. tomatoes
- 1 pound of red kidney beans (seasoned)
- Salt to taste

DIRECTIONS:

Add all ingredients and cook on medium fire (if you use an electric stove, use low setting) for 40 minutes.

. . . .

CHILI

Mrs. Susan Sergeant
Division of Natural Sciences

INGREDIENTS:

- 1 ½ cups of onions
- ½ cup of celery
- ½ cup of bell pepper
- Coarse ground round (3 pounds)
- Tomato sauce (2 #2 cans)
- Cumin
- Chili powder
- 2 teaspoons garlic

DIRECTIONS:

Sauté vegetables and add to browned coarsely chopped round. Add tomato sauce. Simmer slowly for 30 minutes (will burn easily). Add garlic powder, cumin, and chili powder to taste (green chilies may be added as desired). Simmer for an additional 10 minutes, set aside, then serve in edible Taco Tubs with sliced avocado on the side.

SUCCOTASH (Native American)

Mrs. Sylvia Norman Oliver
Clerical Assistant, Humanities

Mrs. Shirley L. Alvis
Clerical Assistant, Natural Sciences

INGREDIENTS:

- 1 to 1 ½ cups of water
- 1 cup of onion
- ½ cup of bell pepper
- 2 pounds of okra
- 2 pounds of corn
- 2 pounds of baby lima beans
- 3 pounds of sweet pickle pork or ham hocks
- 6 fresh tomatoes
- Salt, cayenne pepper, black pepper (season to taste)

"American Indian dish passed down by my mother (Mrs. Florence Galloway Weston-Norman). The dish consists of fresh okra, corn, baby lima beans, stewed tomatoes, and sweet pickle pork or ham hocks."

• •

ROBERT'S PUERTO RICAN HOT TAMALES (CARIBBEAN)

Mrs. Monica Couvertier
(Dr. Patricia Morris' sister)

INGREDIENTS:

- 3 teaspoons of MSG
- 1 cup of chili powder
- 8 teaspoons of Rex minced onion
- 3 teaspoons of Rex garlic powder
- 1 cup of yellow corn meal
- 1 ½ teaspoons of black pepper
- 3 teaspoons of red pepper
- 6 teaspoons of salt
- 2 tablespoons of Rex cayenne
- 1 ¼ cups of water
- 1 can of Rotel and Chives
- 2 (8-ounce) cans of tomato sauce
- 3 pounds of ground round

Gravy:
- 2 cans of tomato sauce
- 1 ounce of chili powder
- 1 can of Rotel sauce
- ½ gallon of water

DIRECTIONS:

Mix ingredients well. Roll filling in cornmeal in wet tamale paper; roll meat in paper. Layer tamales even horizontally and one vertical row. Repeat steps.

For Gravy: Bring water to a boil and add ingredients. Pour mixture over rolled tamales.

In a large Dutch oven or roasting pan, stack the tamales in layers. Cover the tamales with water, then add the seasoned tomato sauce. Cover and simmer for 2 hours on medium heat. Check occasionally, and add water as necessary to keep the tamales covered.

PHEASANT POT PIE (English)

Dr. Gerald Payton
Associate Professor of Chemistry

Dr. Sharon Payton
Food Scientist

INGREDIENTS:

- 1 pheasant
- 2 cups of sifted flour
- 3 teaspoons of baking powder
- ½ tablespoon of salt
- ¾ cup of milk
- ¼ cup of shortening
- 4 tablespoons of tapioca

It consists of biscuits baked on top of pre-cooked deboned pheasant meat in a thickening broth. It is a modification of chicken pot pie and was developed to utilize game harvested by Gerald in Iowa.

DIRECTIONS:

Cook pheasant (whole) in water, cool, and remove meat from bone (cut into 1"–1 ½" cubes and remove any pb shot). Place meat in a 9"x13" pan and pour broth over meat until 1 ½" deep. Sprinkle tapioca over broth and stir. Cook in oven at 400 degrees for 15 minutes.

While cooking the meat-broth-tapioca, prepare biscuits: sift together flour, baking powder, and salt in a bowl. Cut in shortening until mixture resembles coarse crumbs. Make a well, add milk all at once, and stir quickly with a fork until dough follows fork around bowl. Dump dough onto a lightly floured surface and knead gently for 10–12 strokes. Roll dough in pan and bake.

QUICHE LORRAINE (French)

Mrs. Helen W. Beckett
(Dr. Houston's Auntie)

INGREDIENTS:

- 8 ounces of cheddar cheese
- 8 ounces of mozzarella
- 1 small carton of whipping cream
- 4 eggs
- Dash of red pepper
- Dash of sugar
- One onion
- 1 green pepper
- Mushrooms
- Seasonings

DIRECTIONS:

Combine and bake in a pie shell, partially baked (put aluminum foil all over pie crust before baking, so it won't puff. Do not stick pie crust). After 5 minutes take pie crust out of oven. Remove aluminum. Place quiche ingredients in shell. Bake in a 350 degree oven for approximately 40 minutes.

PORK AND SAUREKRAUT (German)

Dr. Ellen Merrill
Assistant Professor of German

INGREDIENTS:

- 5 pounds thin, end-cut pork chops
- Large jar drained, processed sauerkraut
- Large can of tomato sauce
- 5 large onions, peeled and diced
- 1 small bunch of parsley, leaves only
- 5 minced bay leaves
- 2 tablespoons of oregano
- Salt, pepper, Accent (to taste)

DIRECTIONS:

In a large, heavy pan fry pork chops on both sides until lightly browned. Add a little margarine to keep chops from sticking. Cut away from the bone, divide into large bit-sized pieces, and remove all from the pan. Reserve fat. Trim (dice), any marrow, and drippings left in pan. Brown diced onions in this reserve, adding butter or margarine if needed. Add tomato sauce, seasonings, and enough water to form a mixture like spaghetti sauce. Add flour (dissolved in water) to thicken, if necessary.

Add sauerkraut and pork pieces to the mixture. Stir until mixture begins to boil. Reduce heat, cover, and simmer for 20–30 minutes. Uncover, boil away any excess liquid on high heat, stirring constantly. Adjust seasonings. Remove from heat, and let stand until cool. Refrigerate for a day. This recipe is better after it is reheated than served when just finished. Serves 10.

"This is a recipe I found in a manuscript material dating 1834–50 from the settlement named Germantown in north Louisiana, located between Shreveport and Ruston, seven miles outside of Minden. This settlement was formed by pietistic Germans from the Frankfurt area of Germany who migrated to this location because it was on the same geographical latitude with Jerusalem. It has been designated a national historical site and can be visited weekdays, when guided tours are given by descendants of the original colonists. Contact the parish police jury for further information. The original recipe can be duplicated from ingredients found in every supermarket."

GERMAN POTATO SALAD (German)

Mrs. Blanche Cook
Associate Professor of Education

INGREDIENTS:

- 8 large cooked potatoes (diced or sliced)
- 3 stalks of celery, chopped fine
- 2 large red bell peppers (1 ½ chopped fine)
- 6 hard cooked eggs, chopped
- ½ cup of chopped parsley
- 1 teaspoon of mustard
- 2 teaspoons of oil (olive or cooking oil)
- 2 teaspoons of black pepper
- 1 teaspoon of salt
- 1 cup of mayonnaise

DIRECTIONS:

Combine celery, eggs, parsley, mustard, 1 ½ diced red bell pepper, salt, pepper, and mayonnaise. Mix well. Add cooked diced potatoes and mix well. Slice (thin) one half red bell pepper and place over the top. Serve in lettuce leaves.

GERMAN SPRINGERLE COOKIES

Dr. Keith M. Wismar
Assistant Professor of Psychology

INGREDIENTS:

- 2 eggs
- 1 ½ cups of granulated sugar
- Grated rind of 1 lemon
- 1 teaspoon of whole or ground anise seed
- 2 ½ cups of sifted enriched flour
- ½ teaspoon of baking powder
- ½ teaspoon of salt

DIRECTIONS:

Beat eggs until thick and lemon colored. Add sugar gradually, then bean with an electric mixer for 10 minutes. Add flavorings and sifted flour and other dry ingredients. Roll to ¼ inch thickness. Let stand until dry on top. To emboss designs, press floured Springerle rolling pin or board very hard on the dough. Cut around the designs and let dry on board overnight. Remove to a greased cookie sheet and bake in a slow oven (300) for 25–30 minutes. You can buy a Springerle rolling pin at most housewares departments like Maison Blanche.

Springerle are anise-flavored German Christmas cookies. Designs are embossed into the rolled out dough with special rolling pins or boards.

CARROT CAKE

Aisha El-Amin
Division of Nursing

This cake is a favorite of the Muslim community.

INGREDIENTS:

- 4 cups of flour
- 3 eggs
- 2 cups of sugar or honey
- 1 teaspoon of baking soda
- 1 teaspoon of cinnamon
- 1 ½ cups of vegetable oil
- 1 cup of nuts
- 2 teaspoons of vanilla extract
- 2 cups of grated carrots
- 1 small can of crushed unsweetened pineapple

DIRECTIONS:

Blend sugar, oil, and eggs, then add vanilla. In a separate bowl combine flour, baking soda, baking powder, and cinnamon. Add dry mix to sugar, oil, vanilla, eggs, baking soda, and baking powder. Blend but do not over blend. Fold in nuts, carrots, and pineapples. Bake at 250 degrees for 1 hour and 20 minutes. You can add a glaze of your choice.

· ·

FRUIT CAKE

Mrs. Helen W. Beckett
Dillard Auxiliary Supporter
Dallas, TX

INGREDIENTS:

- 4 cups of flour
- 1 pound of candied cherries
- 1 pound of candied pineapple
- 1 pound of pecans
- 1 pound of citrons
- 1 pound of butter
- 1 pound of raisins
- 1 pound of currants
- 2 teaspoons of baking powder
- 1 teaspoon of cinnamon
- 1 teaspoon of allspice
- 1 teaspoon of nutmeg
- 11 eggs
- 1 cup of strong black coffee
- 1 cup of black molasses

DIRECTIONS:

Cut all fruits and mix with flour containing all dry ingredients. Be sure to mix flour and fruit well. Add butter melted in a pan with coffee and molasses. Stir liquids into flour and fruit mixture. Beat eggs and add to molasses and coffee. Pour in a greased pan lined with foil.

Place in an oven with a low flame (200 degrees) for 4 hours. Makes one large and one small cake (or several 2-pound cakes). Pull paper off while it's warm. Put Bourbon in by the tablespoon until moist.

MONKEY BREAD

Mrs. Sylvia F. Cook
Dillard Auxiliary Founder

INGREDIENTS:

- 1 pound of butter
- 3 eggs
- ½ cup of sugar or 1 cup (for sweetness)
- 3 yeast packages
- 1 cup of milk
- 6 cups of flour
- 1 teaspoon of salt

The original monkey bread recipe was first prepared by Mrs. Daisy Young who has shared her favorite recipe with Mrs. Cook. Mrs. Cook's monkey bread has become a traditional favorite at the International Food Festival.

DIRECTIONS:

Scald milk, add 1 stick of butter, salt, and sugar. Mix well. Dissolve yeast in ¼ cup of warm water. Add to milk and butter solution. Add eggs. Beat in an electric mixer or by hand. Add flour a cup at a time. Unless you have a heavy duty mixer, you will have to mix by hand after you have added 3 cups of flour. Continue adding flour until the dough can be kneaded by hand. Knead for 10 minutes. Grease top with a little oil and cover and let rise in a warm place for about 2 or 3 hours. When dough has doubled its bulk, punch down and roll out on a floured board until it is ¼ inch thick. Melt the other 3 sticks of butter. Cut the dough in diamond shapes and dip each piece completely in melted butter. Lay around in a molded pan. Stagger rows. Makes 4 rows, cover again and let it rise until it has doubled its bulk. Bake in a 400 degree oven for 25 minutes. Remove from oven and turn upside down on a platter. Serve at once. Sometimes I add raisins to the first mixture before letting it rise.

• •

OKIE CHOCOLATE CAKE

Ms. Florence Lyons
Assistant Professor of Drama

CAKE:

- 2 cups of Pillsbury's Best All Purpose Unbleached Flour
- 2 cups of sugar
- 1 ¼ teaspoons of baking soda
- 1 teaspoon of salt
- ½ teaspoon of baking powder
- 1 cup of water
- ¾ cup of dairy sour cream
- ¼ cup of shortening
- 1 teaspoon of vanilla
- 2 eggs
- 4 ounces (4 squares) unsweetened chocolate, melted and cooled

FROSTING:

- 3 cups of powdered sugar
- ¼ cup of dairy sour cream
- ¼ cup of margarine or butter, softened
- 3 tablespoons of milk
- 1 teaspoon of vanilla

LUSSEKATTER (Swedish Letter Buns)

Mrs. Helen Malin
Assistant Professor of English

INGREDIENTS:

- ½ cup (¼ pound) butter or margarine
- ¾ cup whipping cream or milk
- ⅓ cup of sugar
- ½ teaspoon of salt
- 1 teaspoon of ground cardamom or ¹⁄₁₆ teaspoon ground saffron
- 1 package of active dry yeast
- ¼ cup of warm (110 to 115 degrees) water
- About 4 cups of all-purpose flour
- 1 egg
- About ⅓ cup of raisins
- 1 egg yolk mixed with 1 tablespoon of water

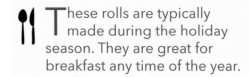

These rolls are typically made during the holiday season. They are great for breakfast any time of the year.

DIRECTIONS:

In a 1 or 2 quart pan, melt butter; remove from heat and stir in cream, sugar, salt, and cardamom (or saffron). Let cool to lukewarm. In the large bowl of an electric mixer, blend yeast with warm water; let stand 5 minutes to soften. Add the cooled cream mixture, egg, and 2 cups of flour. Mix until blended, then beat at medium speed for 2 minutes longer. With a spoon, gradually stir in about 1 ½ cups more of flour to make a stiff dough.

Turn dough out on a floured board and knead until smooth and elastic, about 10 minutes, adding flour to board as needed to prevent sticking. Place dough in a greased bowl, turning to grease top. Cover bowl with plastic wrap and let dough rise in a warm place until doubled, about 1 ½ hours.

Punch dough down. To shape rolls, divide dough into 24 equal-size pieces; roll each piece on a flat surface with your palm to make a rope about 9 inches long. Coil ends of rope in opposite directions to make an S shape. Push a raisin deep into the center of each coil.

Place rolls at least 2 inches apart on greased baking sheets. Cover with plastic wrap and let rolls rise in a warm place until puffy, about 45 minutes. Brush rolls with the egg yolk mixture. Bake on the middle racks of 375 degree oven for 15 minutes or until rolls are golden brown on bottom and lightly browned around edges (reverse pan positions if necessary for even browning). Serve hot; or cool, cover with plastic wrap, and store at room temperature 1 day; freeze for longer storage. To reheat, place on baking sheet, cover with foil, and set in a 375 degree oven for 10 minutes. Makes 2 dozen rolls.

VIENNESE TORTE

Mrs. Helen Malin
Assistant Professor of English

INGREDIENTS:

- 2 ounces unsweetened chocolate
- 3 tablespoons of salad oil
- ¼ teaspoon salt
- ½ cup of hot strong coffee
- 1 cup of sugar
- 1 egg
- ¼ cup of buttermilk
- 1 teaspoon each soda and vanilla
- 1 cup of all-purpose flour
- ½ cup of apricot preserves
- 2 tablespoons of brandy or 1 teaspoon extract
- Chocolate frosting (recipe follows)

DIRECTIONS:

In the top of a double boiler, stir chocolate, oil, salt, and coffee over barely simmering water until blended. Pour mixture into the large bowl of an electric mixer and add sugar, egg, buttermilk, soda, and vanilla; beat on medium speed until well blended.

Add flour and continue beating for 5 minutes, occasionally scraping down with a rubber spatula. Pour into a greased and floured 8-inch cake pan. Bake in a 350 degree oven just until cake begins to pull from sides of pan, about 30 minutes. Set on a rack to cool, then remove from pan. (If you like, wrap cool cake and freeze as long as 1 week. Thaw uncovered, at room temperature before proceeding).

Cut cake in half horizontally to make 2 layers. Combine apricot preserves and brandy; spread evenly over bottom layer of cake. Set top layer in place and put cake on a rack. Slowly pour chocolate frosting onto center of cake so it flows over the entire surface. With a spatula, guide icing down over sides of the cake to coat smoothly. Chill until the icing is set, at least 30 minutes. Using a wide spatula, loosen cake from rack and gently slide onto a serving plate. (If cake is made ahead, cover without touching and chill up to 6 hours; return to room temperature to serve). Makes about 10 servings.

For Chocolate frosting: In the top of a double boiler over barely simmering water, stir 5 squares (5 ounces) semisweet baking chocolate and 4 teaspoons of solid vegetable shortening until melted.

APPLE BROWN BETTY WITH HARD SAUCE

Linda G. Nash
Division of Nursing

INGREDIENTS:

- 2 cups of stale breadcrumbs
- 6 cups sliced apples
- ½ cup of sugar
- ¼ teaspoon of cinnamon
- ¼ teaspoon of salt
- 3 tablespoons of lemon juice
- ¼ cup of water
- 2 tablespoons of butter

Hard Sauce:

- ½ cup of butter
- 1 ⅔ cups of powdered sugar
- 1 teaspoon of vanilla or
    1 ½ teaspoons of sherry or brandy

DIRECTIONS:

Put ⅓ crumbs into a buttered casserole dish and cover with 3 cups of apples. Combine the sugar, cinnamon, and salt; sprinkle half of the sugar mixture over the apples. Add another layer of crumbs and apples; sprinkle with the remainder of the sugar mixture. Top with crumbs and pour lemon and water over pudding then dot with butter. Cover dish and bake for 30 minutes at 350 degrees. Uncover and bake for 15 minutes longer. Serve hot with Hard Sauce.

For Sauce: Cream butter until soft and smooth. Alternately stir in sugar with salt and flavoring. Mixture should be stiff when completed. Chill until hard. Cut into slices and serve over warm dessert.

 Apple Brown Betty is a pudding made with fresh apples and served with hard sauce. It is a perfect holiday dessert treat.

PECAN PIE

Ms. Beryl Segre
Assistant Professor and Coordinator of
Public Health/Allied Health Programs

INGREDIENTS:

- 3 egg whites
- 1 cup of granulated sugar
- 1 ½ teaspoons of vanilla
- ¾ cup of rolled graham crackers
- ¾ cup of chopped pecans

DIRECTIONS:

Mix together, put mixture in a buttered pie plate. Bake for 30 minutes at 300 degrees.

SWEET POTATO PIE DELIGHT

Mrs. Debra Surtain
Mass Communication Office

INGREDIENTS:

- 4–5 large sweet potatoes
- 1 can of cream
- ½ stick of butter
- Dash of salt
- 2 cups of sugar (add or to taste)
- 1 tablespoon of cinnamon
- 1 tablespoon of nutmeg
- 1 tablespoon of vanilla
- 4 eggs
- Unbaked pie shell

DIRECTIONS:

Boil potatoes whole (with skin on) until tender. Peel skin off and place potatoes in a large mixing bowl and mash. Add sugar, salt, nutmeg , and cinnamon. Mix in butter, cream, and vanilla. Add the eggs, then blend until creamy. Heat oven to 350 degrees and bake until golden brown (approximately 30–35 minutes).

 "A family tradition passed down from my great-grandmother of Creole origin.

LARRY'S MUNCHY PECAN PIE

Lawrence R. Williams Sr.
Division of Natural Sciences

INGREDIENTS:

- 3 eggs, slightly beaten
- 1 cup of sugar
- 1 cup of Karo light or dark syrup
- 2 tablespoons margarine
    or butter, melted
- 1 teaspoon of vanilla
- 1 ½ cups of pecans
- 1 unbaked (9") pie shell

DIRECTIONS:

In a large bowl stir in the first five ingredients until well blended. Stir in pecans. Pour into pie shell. Bake in a 350 degree oven for 1 hour or until center holds together and is not runny. Cool. Serves 8 or makes 8 miniature pies.

PECAN BRITTLE

Mrs. Daisy Young
Dillard Auxiliary Supporter

INGREDIENTS:

- 2 cups of sugar
- 1 cup of white corn syrup
- ¼ cup of water
- 3 cups of pecan halves
- 2 tablespoons of butter
- 1 tablespoon of baking soda

DIRECTIONS:

In a heavy saucepan heat sugar, syrup, and water until it boils. Add nuts. Stir constantly. Cook until syrup spins a thread. Add butter and soda. Beat rapidly and pour in a buttered pan spreading to ¼-inch thickness. When cold, break into pieces. Peanut Brittle can be made from same recipe. Add 4 cups raw peanuts with skin and ½ cup of water.

Fair Dillard: A Collection of Contemporary Recipes
President Walter M. Kimbrough, 2012–

My, how times have changed since the first edition of the Dillard University Cookbook! With the increase in the number of families with two working parents, the onslaught of extracurricular activities for our children, and the frantic busyness and pace of our lives today, many Americans find themselves grabbing dinner out of a drive-thru window and eating it in their cars. As a working mom myself, I must admit that my own children, Lydia and Benjamin, have eaten more than their fair share of chicken fingers and French fries in the back seat of my car. When meals are prepared at home, changing gender roles have resulted in as many men as women "bringing home the bacon and frying it up in a pan," to recall the iconic 1980s Enjoli perfume commercial. I know that my husband, even as President of Dillard University, does far more cooking than my father or his ever did.

I did not grow up learning how to cook. In fact, it was not until I was married, with two children of my own, that I really appreciated the value of a home cooked meal. The year 2008 was the first Christmas holiday that we did not travel to Mobile or Atlanta to visit extended family and to enjoy the comforts of a home cooked meal prepared by someone else. Benjamin was just a month old and we decided he was too young to travel. Confronted with the task of preparing a holiday meal on my own, my father jokingly said to me, "So, what are you going to do? Order take-out for Christmas?" Mortified by the idea of my children eating Christmas dinner out of plastic containers, and emboldened by the challenge my father had unknowingly placed before me, I feverishly began to gather recipes. The result? Cornish hens, green beans, wild rice, pound cake, and the beginning of wonderful memories where good food has brought my family and friends together.

Thanks to the help of recipes like the ones you will find in this cookbook, I gained a newfound confidence and interest in the culinary arts. As a result, my children do not remember a time when I did not bake their birthday cakes each year, and we have many fond memories around the kitchen, usually in-

volving Lydia and Benjamin trying to lick cake batter out of a bowl! Food and cooking continue to bring people together.

In my own family, preparing Thanksgiving dinner for Dillard University students has become one of our favorite traditions, and an invaluable way to build community with Dillard students. Dillard University, through its Ray Charles Program in African-American Material Culture is preserving the culinary traditions and culture of African-Americans in New Orleans and the South. It is my hope that this commemorative edition of the Dillard University Cookbook will continue our culinary traditions with recipes to create the food that will help you build community wherever you are.

Eat well.

Mrs. Adria Nobles Kimbrough

CHEF JOYNELL'S
CRAWFISH BREAD

INGREDIENTS:

- 1 loaf of French bread
- 2 tablespoons of butter
- 2 tablespoons of all-purpose flour
- 1 cup of milk
- 1 cup of heavy cream
- ¼ cup of grated parmesan cheese
- Onion and garlic powder and Tony Chachere's
- 1 pound of peeled crawfish
- 1 bunch of green onions, chopped
- 3 cups of shredded mozzarella cheese

DIRECTIONS:

In a small saucepan melt the butter or margarine over a low heat and whisk in the flour until smooth and cook for about 5 minutes. Combine the milk and cream and slowly whisk into the roux, bring to a simmer and season to taste with the onion powder, granulated garlic, and Tony's, be careful with the Tony's, it contains a lot of salt, or you can substitute a salt-free Creole seasoning. Simmer until thick, the sauce is ready when it can coat the back of a metal spoon. Add the crawfish with the juice, the green onion, and parmesan cheese. Stir sauce to blend the ingredients and remove from heat. Cut the loaf of French bread in half lengthwise, place on a baking sheet pan and spoon the sauce liberally on both sides of the bread. Cover both pieces of bread with the grated mozzarella cheese and bake in a 350 oven until cheese is melted and bubbling. Let the bread cool for a few minutes then cut into 3" slices and serve.

Dillard Dining Services in Kearny Dining Hall feeds hundreds of students, faculty, staff, and members of the community daily. Many Dillard University alumni have fond memories of Monday red beans and rice day and Friday fish fry. For students and faculty not from New Orleans, they are invited to experience a taste of New Orleans that embodies a culture of hospitality and tradition. The communal warm setting invites everyone to the table to break bread.

DAUBE GLACÉ

Mrs. Leah Chase & Edgar "Dook" Chase IV
New Orleans, LA
Dooky Chase Restaurant, Dook's Place Restaurant

INGREDIENTS:

- Leftover beef roast 2–3 pounds (remove bones)
- 1 green bell pepper, minced
- 1 yellow onion, minced
- 2 carrots, minced
- 2 cloves of garlic, minced
- Dash of cayenne pepper
- Salt and pepper
- 2 sprigs of chopped thyme
- Knox unflavored gelatin (3 packets)
- 1 teaspoon of red pepper flakes

DIRECTIONS:

Chop leftover beef roast finely. Chop all vegetables finely (¼ cup each). Save the liquid from the roast. Simmer in liquid in a pot for ten minutes. Add seasoning and vegetables. Simmer on medium low heat for ten minutes. In a separate pot follow gelatin directions and bring to a boil. Mix all ingredients thoroughly together. Grease a mold for the daube glacé. Add the meat mixture to the mold and refrigerate overnight. Serve with a good French bread, crackers, or pepper jelly.

Daube Glacé is a classic 19th-century New Orleans Creole dish. It is served like pâté. However, the old Creoles would serve daube glacé for breakfast over grits.

OYSTER PATTIES

Zella Palmer
New Orleans, LA
Chair, Dillard University Ray Charles Program

INGREDIENTS:

- 4 dozen oysters with liquid
- 1 medium onion, diced
- 2 tablespoons of chopped fresh parsley
- 1 tablespoon of flour
- 2 tablespoons of butter
- ¼ teaspoon of lemon juice
- ½ cup of chopped mushrooms
- Salt and pepper
- Dash of cayenne pepper
- 12 small pastry shells

DIRECTIONS:

Chop oysters. Cook 2 dozen oysters in their liquid by bringing them to a quick boil. Add butter in saucepan, chopped onion, and add flour slowly. Add remaining ingredients and the other two dozen oysters. Season to taste. Cook for 6 minutes, then pour into pastry shells. Bake in 425 degrees for 15 minutes.

OYSTER LOAF

Zella Palmer
New Orleans, LA
Chair, Dillard University Ray Charles Program

INGREDIENTS:

- 2 dozen oysters
- 1 loaf of good French bread
- 2 tablespoons of butter
- 1 cup of milk
- 1 egg
- 1 cup of cornmeal or cracker meal
- Salt and pepper to taste
- Cooking oil

DIRECTIONS:

Preheat oven to 400 degrees. Cut the French bread in half and remove the insides of the bread. Slather butter on the inside and outside of the bread. In a frying pan, heat oil on medium-high heat. Make an egg wash in a deep dish of milk, egg, salt, and pepper. In a separate bowl, add cornmeal. Drain oysters and pat dry with a paper towel. One by one dip the oysters in the egg wash and roll gently in the cornmeal. Fry oysters until golden brown and crispy. Toast buttered French bread in the oven. Fill toasted loaf with fried oysters. Serve with lemon wedges and hot sauce.

GRILLADES

Zella Palmer
New Orleans, LA
Chair, Dillard University Ray Charles Program

INGREDIENTS:

- 3 beef round steaks
- 2 tablespoons of shortening or oil
- 1 green bell pepper, minced
- 1 large onion, thinly sliced
- 2 cups of chopped Creole tomatoes
- 1 bunch of chopped fresh or dried parsley
- 1 garlic clove, minced
- 1 cup of hot water
- Salt and pepper to taste
- 1 cup of flour

DIRECTIONS:

In a pan, heat shortening or oil to medium-high heat. Season beef round steak. Brown beef round steak in shortening. Remove from skillet. Add flour to the pan and brown lightly. Add the onions and sauté until light brown. Stir in tomatoes, green pepper, parsley, garlic, salt, and pepper. Place beef round steaks in the pan, pour hot water, cover, and cook slowly until the steak is fork tender (1 ½ to 2 hours). Serve with cooked rice. Garnish with parsley.

SHRIMP CREOLE

Zella Palmer
New Orleans, LA
Chair, Dillard University Ray Charles Program

INGREDIENTS:

- 2 pounds of fresh shrimp, peeled and deveined
- 1 large onion, minced
- 2 tablespoons of green bell pepper, diced
- 1 can of tomato sauce (8 ounces)
- 1 tablespoon of flour
- 1 garlic clove, minced
- 1 teaspoon of pepper
- 1 teaspoon of salt
- 1 tablespoon of butter
- Dash of cayenne
- Pinch of fresh thyme
- 1 ½ to 2 cans of water
- Pinch of sugar

DIRECTIONS:

Sauté onion in butter until tender on medium heat. Stir in garlic, green bell pepper. Sauté for 2 minutes. Blend in flour. Season with salt, pepper, thyme, sugar, and cayenne. Add tomato sauce and simmer for 5 minutes. Stir in water. Bring to a low boil and add shrimp. Cover for 15 minutes.

• •

LOUISIANA PEPPER JELLY SWEET AND SPICY WINGS

Zella Palmer
New Orleans, LA
Chair, Dillard University Ray Charles Program

INGREDIENTS:

- 12 wings
- 2 tablespoons of Louisiana pepper jelly
- 1 small bottle of hot sauce (Crystal preferably)
- 1 stick of butter
- 1 ½ cups of flour
- 2 eggs
- 2 tablespoons of Creole or Cajun seasoning
- Vegetable or canola oil
- Ranch dressing (optional)
- ½ cup of cracker meal

DIRECTIONS:

Rinse wings in cold water. Set aside. In a bowl or large paper bag mix flour and seasoning. Make an egg wash in a deep dish. Heat oil in a deep frying pan at medium-high heat. Dredge wings in egg wash and then the flour and cracker meal. While the chicken is frying, simmer butter and 1 bottle of hot sauce on low-medium heat in a pan. Add 2 tablespoons of Louisiana pepper jelly. Whisk and cook for 3 minutes. Set aside. When the chicken wings are fried to a golden brown, remove and drain oil on thick paper towels. In a separate bowl, add fried chicken wings and pour hot sauce mixture over the wings. Make sure the fried wings are covered well with the sauce. Serve wings with ranch dressing (optional).

VEAL PANEE (BREADED VEAL)

Zella Palmer
New Orleans, LA
Chair, Dillard University Ray Charles Program

INGREDIENTS:

- 6 thin veal steaks
- ½ cup of plain breadcrumbs
- 1 egg, beaten
- ½ cup of flour
- ⅓ cup of dried parsley
- Shortening or oil
- Lemon wedges (optional)
- Salt and pepper to taste

DIRECTIONS:

Coat veal steaks with flour, salt, dried parsley, and pepper. Dip veal into an egg wash then coat with plain breadcrumbs. Heat shortening or oil in a deep skillet on medium-high heat. Sauté on both sides until golden brown and crispy. Serve with lemon wedges.

NEW ORLEANS BARBECUE SHRIMP

Zella Palmer
New Orleans, LA
Chair, Dillard University Ray Charles Program

INGREDIENTS:

- 6 pounds of jumbo sized shrimp (Louisiana preferably)
- 2 sticks of butter
- 1 sprig of fresh rosemary, chopped
- 2 tablespoons of brown sugar
- 1 tablespoon of smoked paprika
- 1 teaspoon of Creole seasoning
- 1 teaspoon of crab boil
- 2 lemons
- ⅓ cup of fresh parsley, chopped
- French bread

DIRECTIONS:

Preheat oven to 325 degrees. Leave heads and tails on shrimp. Rinse any grit off the shrimp. In a cast iron sauce pan, melt 2 sticks of butter at medium heat. Add smoked paprika, Creole seasoning, rosemary, and crab boil to butter. Add shrimp and constantly baste with infused butter. When shrimp turn completely pink. Finish in the oven for 8 minutes. Remove. Squeeze a little lemon over the cooked shrimp and garnish with fresh parsley. Serve with French bread and lemon wedges.

SAUTEED DEER TENLERLOINS

Anthony Bennett, Marrero, LA
Public Health Major, Class of 2018
Dillard University Ray Charles Program Scholarship Recipient

INGREDIENTS:

- 2 deer tenderloins
- 1 large onion, chopped
- 1 small green bell pepper, minced
- 1 stick of butter
- Vinegar (optional)
- 9 ounces of chicken or beef stock or water
- Favorite seasoning

DIRECTIONS:

Wash deer tenderloins well. Add ¼ cup of white vinegar to deer tenderloins in a bowl. Allow the tenderloins to marinate for ten minutes. Remove tenderloins from the bowl and wash off the vinegar. Pat the meat dry. Season with salt, black pepper, garlic, and onion powder or favorite seasoning. Marinate tenderloins for 30 minutes or overnight. Finely chop 1 onion and a green bell pepper. In a large skillet, melt butter on medium low heat. Add the chopped onion and green bell pepper. Cook until onions are softened. Add the tenderloins and brown on both sides. After browning the tenderloins, add 9 ounces of chicken or beef broth or water. Simmer for about 30 minutes on low-medium heat. Do not overcook the meat.

CHARGRILLED OYSTERS

Miss Linda Green "Yakamein Lady"
New Orleans, LA
New Orleans Soul Food Company

INGREDIENTS:

- 2 dozen large fresh Louisiana oysters (shucked on the half shell)
- 2 sticks of salted butter
- Creole seasoning to taste
- 5 tablespoons of grated parmesan cheese
- 2 tablespoons of dried parsley
- Good French bread
- Lemon wedges

DIRECTIONS:

In a bowl, mix melted butter, seasoning, parsley and parmesan cheese. On a very hot grill, grill oysters for a few minutes until the oyster meat starts to curl. Drizzle sauce over the oysters while they are cooking. Add a little more parmesan cheese and grill oysters until the cheese is golden brown. Remove. Serve with French bread and lemon wedges.

STUFFED VEAL POCKET WITH OYSTER DRESSING

Miss Linda Green "Yakamein Lady"
New Orleans, LA
New Orleans Soul Food Company

INGREDIENTS:

- 1 veal leg roast (deboned by a butcher)
- ⅓ cup of Creole seasoning

OYSTER DRESSING

- 2 loaves of stale French bread
- ¼ quart of fresh oysters in liquid
- 2 sticks of salted butter
- Salt and pepper
- Creole seasoning
- ½ cup of water
- 1 finely chopped green bell pepper
- 2 stalks of finely chopped celery
- 1 finely chopped sweet onion
- ¼ cup of chopped fresh parsley

DIRECTIONS:

Season veal leg roast and marinate overnight. Preheat oven at 350 degrees. Stuff the veal pocket with oyster dressing. Tie roast with a string or sew the meat closed. Puncture the veal pocket with a sharp small knife 5 times. Place the veal pocket in a roasting pan with a cup of water at the bottom roaster. Cover the veal pocket and cook for 2 hours at 350 degrees. Baste often.

For Dressing: In a large mixing bowl. Crumble two stale loaves of French bread. Set aside. Remove oysters from liquid. Reserve oyster liquid. Chop oysters in small chunks. Set aside. In a pan, sauté chopped green bell pepper, celery, fresh parsley, and an onion with two sticks of butter on low-medium heat until softened. Season with salt and pepper. Set aside. Add oyster liquid to crumbled French bread. Mix with hands. Add ½ cup of water. Mix. Add oysters and then cooked vegetable mixture (Holy Trinity). Mix with hands. Season to taste.

SMOTHERED TURKEY NECKS AND RICE

Miss Linda Green "Yakamein Lady"
New Orleans, LA
New Orleans Soul Food Company

INGREDIENTS:

- 5 pounds of turkey necks
- Salt and pepper
- 1 cup of flour
- 1 chopped green bell pepper
- 1 chopped sweet onion
- 2 teaspoons of celery salt
- ⅓ cup of fresh chopped parsley
- ⅓ cup of oil

DIRECTIONS:

In a large boiling pot, bring water to a boil, enough to fit 5 pounds of turkey necks. Add salt to water. Boil turkey necks for 2 hours on medium heat until tender. Remove turkey necks from the water; set aside. In a sauté pan, make a roux. Heat pan to medium heat, add oil, and whisk in flour slowly. Add the chopped onion, fresh parsley, and bell pepper. Season with celery salt and pepper. Season to taste. Cook until gravy consistency. Pour gravy over the turkey necks. Serve with cooked rice and cornbread.

RED BEANS AND RICE

Miss Linda Green "Yakamein Lady"
New Orleans, LA
New Orleans Soul Food Company

INGREDIENTS:

- 1 pound of red beans (Camelia)
- ¼ cup of minced garlic
- 1 cup of red, yellow, green bell pepper, diced and seeds removed
- 1 small white onion, minced
- 1 red onion, minced
- 1 cup of fresh chopped parsley
- 2 cups of chopped celery
- 1 gallon of water to cover red beans
- 4 cups of cooked sausage (D & D sausage)
- Cooked white rice
- ¼ cup of Creole seasoning
- 1 bay leaf

DIRECTIONS:

Wash beans. Put your water in a large pot and bring to a boil. Add seasoning. Add chopped celery, peppers, onion, and bay leaf. Chop smoked sausage. Let red beans cook for 45 minutes. When the red beans get semi-soft, add the smoked sausage. Cook for another hour. Season to taste. Serve over cooked rice and garnish with fresh parsley or chopped green onions.

STUFFED BELL PEPPERS

Miss Linda Green "Yakamein Lady"
New Orleans, LA
New Orleans Soul Food Company

INGREDIENTS:

- 4 green bell peppers
    (cut in halves, seeds removed)
- 1 pound of ground beef
- 2 pounds of small uncooked shrimp
- Salt and pepper
- 1 cup of plain breadcrumbs
- 2 eggs
- 1 green bell pepper, finely chopped
- 1 medium onion, finely chopped
- 1 stalk of celery, finely chopped

DIRECTIONS:

Preheat oven to 350 degrees. Season ground meat with salt and pepper. Sauté until browned. Add the bell pepper, onion, and celery. Add shrimp. Cook until the ground meat is cooked and is in a crumble like consistency. Set aside. Do not drain the meat and shrimp mixture. Cut in half and remove seeds and tops from 6 green bell peppers. Set aside. In a mixing bowl, add meat and shrimp mixture. Mix in two eggs. Mix in plain breadcrumbs. Season to taste. Spoon the meat and shrimp mixture into the halved bell peppers. The meat and shrimp mixture should just cover the rim of the bell pepper. Sprinkle tops of stuffed bell peppers with breadcrumbs. Add a little water to the bottom of a pan. Place stuffed bell peppers in the pan. Cover pan tightly with aluminum foil. Cook for 25 minutes or until the bell peppers are tender.

CORNBREAD

Mary Louise Thomas, Bayou Lafourche, LA
Former Chef and Owner
New Orleans Mais Oui: Creole & Soul Food Restaurant

INGREDIENTS:

- ¼ cup of Crisco
- 1 cup of yellow cornmeal
- ⅔ cup of flour
- 1 or 2 teaspoons of sugar (optional)
- 2 eggs
- 2 teaspoons of baking powder
- 2 cups of milk

DIRECTIONS:

Preheat oven to 350 degrees. Mix all ingredients well in a mixing bowl. Pour cornbread mixture into a greased baking pan. Place pan in oven for 45 minutes or until bread is golden brown or until a fork inserted into the center of the pan comes out clean. Serve warm.

The cornbread at Mais Oui in New Orleans was to die for in the 1980s. Cornbread lovers never could get enough.

CRAWFISH BISQUE

Mary Louise Thomas, Bayou Lafourche, LA
Former Chef and Owner
New Orleans Mais Oui: Creole & Soul Food Restaurant

INGREDIENTS:

- Crawfish heads
- 2 pounds of peeled crawfish tails
- 1 ½ cups of onions, chopped
- ¾ cup of green onions, chopped
- ½ cup of celery, chopped
- 1 medium green bell pepper, chopped
- ⅓ cup of parsley, chopped
- 1 cup of plain breadcrumbs
- ½ cup of seafood or chicken stock
- 2 eggs, beaten
- Salt and pepper to taste
- ¼ cup of flour

Roux

- 4 tablespoons of butter
- 2 tablespoons of flour
- 1 quart of seafood or chicken stock

DIRECTIONS:

Preheat oven to 400 degrees. Chop seasonings very fine. Combine one cup of chopped crawfish tail meat with seasonings. Blend in breadcrumbs and seafood or chicken stock. Gently cook mixture over medium heat for about 10 minutes. Add salt and pepper to taste. Add the eggs to cooled crawfish tails. Stuff the mixture into clean crawfish heads. Sprinkle stuffed heads lightly with flour. Place stuffed heads on a baking sheet. Bake for 20 minutes in a 400 degree pre-heated oven.

To make a roux, first you melt butter in a large iron pot over medium heat. Sprinkle flour, stirring constantly. Continue to stir flour and butter until flour turns a rich brown color. Thin flour and butter paste slowly with seafood or chicken stock. Add crawfish tails and stuffed crawfish heads to the roux. Simmer ½ hour stirring gently. Garnish with parsley. Serve over a generous portion of rice.

JAMBALAYA

Mary Louise Thomas, Bayou Lafourche, LA
Former Chef and Owner
New Orleans Mais Oui: Creole & Soul Food Restaurant

INGREDIENTS:

- 1 stick of butter or margarine
- 1 cup of onions, chopped medium fine
- 1 cup of green onions, chopped medium fine
- 1 cup of celery, chopped medium fine
- 1 cup of green bell pepper, chopped fine
- 6 chicken breasts precooked
- 1 pound of peeled and deveined shrimp
- 6 garlic cloves, chopped medium fine
- 1 can of tomato puree (13 ounces)
- 1 tablespoon of Worcestershire sauce
- 4 bay leaves
- 5 cups of cooked long grain rice
- 1 pound of chopped smoked sausage
- 1 tablespoon of basil
- 1 tablespoon of brown sugar
- 1 teaspoon of cayenne pepper
- 4 ½ cups of chicken stock

DIRECTIONS:

Chop all seasonings medium fine. Melt butter (or margarine) in a large iron pot or Dutch oven set over medium heat. Put seasoning in pot, including tomato puree. Sauté stirring constantly until well mixed and the seasonings are tender. Add Worcestershire sauce, bay leaves, basil, brown sugar, cayenne, chicken stock, salt, and pepper. Allow to simmer on medium heat for 1 hour, stirring occasionally. Add the steamed chicken and cooked rice (shrimp and sausage) continuing to simmer for another ½ hour.

REDFISH COURTBOUILLON

Mary Louise Thomas, Bayou Lafourche, LA
Former Chef and Owner
New Orleans Mais Oui: Creole & Soul Food Restaurant

INGREDIENTS:

- 6 large fillets of redfish or catfish
- 2 teaspoons of salt
- 1 teaspoon of pepper
- ½ teaspoon of cayenne pepper
- 1 stick of butter

Courtbouillion Sauce

- 1 can of stewed tomatoes (16 ounces)
- ½ cup of green bell pepper, chopped
- 1 can of tomato sauce (16 ounces)
- 8 garlic cloves, minced
- 1 can of seafood or chicken broth (16 ounces)
- 4 bay leaves, crushed
- 1 cup of onion, chopped
- 1 teaspoon of Zatarain's crab shrimp boil
- 1 cup of celery, chopped
- 1 stick of butter
- 1 cup of green onion, chopped
- Salt and pepper to taste
- ½ cup of parsley, chopped
- 1 sprig of fresh thyme

DIRECTIONS:

Preheat oven to 350 degrees. Wash and dry fillets. Lightly grease a baking pan with butter. Place the fillets in the pan. Combine the salt, pepper, and cayenne and sprinkle mixture evenly over the fish. Sprinkle a little butter on top of the fish to prevent the fillets from drying. Seal or cover the dish tightly. Bake for 15 minutes in the oven.

For Sauce: Chop all seasonings medium fine. Melt butter in a stockpot or Dutch oven. Add chopped seasonings and sauté about 2 minutes until butter is absorbed into the vegetables. Add stewed tomatoes and tomato sauce, stirring to blend with seasonings. Add seafood or chicken broth, Zatarain's Crab & Shrimp Boil, crushed bay leaves, and fresh chopped thyme. Simmer on low heat for approximately 1 ½ hours, stirring occasionally.

Prior to serving, place pre-cooked fillets gently into sauce so that they don't break up. Heat sauce until ingredients are hot being careful not to boil the sauce or cook it again.

Cook enough rice for the meal. To serve, place rice in bottom of dish. Top with fish fillet. Spoon courtbouillon sauce over rice and catfish fillets. The Courtbouillon Sauce can be prepared ahead of time. It tastes better after sitting overnight in the refrigerator.

OYSTER AND ARTICHOKE SOUP

Beverly McKenna
New Orleans, LA
McKenna Publishing Company

INGREDIENTS:

- ½ pound butter or margarine
- 1 cup flour
- ½ bunch fresh parsley, chopped
- 1 ½ cups of chopped green onions
- 6 cloves of garlic, chopped fine
- 3 cans artichoke heart quarters, plain
- 6 teaspoons instant chicken bouillon
- 2 quarts scalded milk
- 2 quarts oysters with liquid
- Salt, to taste
- White pepper
- Dash of Tabasco sauce
- Worcestershire sauce

DIRECTIONS:

Melt butter, add flour, cook on low heat for ten minutes. Do not brown the butter. Add chopped green onions, fresh chopped parsley, garlic, 3 cans of artichoke hearts, brine water, and chicken bouillon (6 cubes or 6 teaspoons). Add 2 quarts scalded milk. Simmer until very hot, but do not allow milk to boil. Add 2 quarts of oysters with liquid (cook until their edges begin to curl –4 to 5 minutes). Keep temperature medium to high without letting mixture boil (too high will curdle milk and toughen oysters). Add salt to taste and white pepper. Add Tabasco sauce and Worcestershire sauce.

THANKSGIVING LEFTOVER TURKEY BONE GUMBO

Liz Williams, New Orleans, LA
Director and Founder,
Southern Food & Beverage Museum

INGREDIENTS:

- ¼ cup flour
- ¼ cup oil or bacon fat or duck fat
- 2 large onions, chopped
- 1 bunch scallions, chopped
- 3 stalks of celery, chopped
- 1 large green bell pepper, chopped
- Garlic, minced, at least 3 cloves
- 3 smoked sausage links, chopped
- Gravy from Thanksgiving turkey
- Turkey carcass, including any vegetables
- Water or broth or wine
- Bay leaf or two
- Salt and pepper
- 1 tablespoon grated lemon rind
- Leftover turkey meat
- 1 sprig of thyme
- Bunch of fresh parsley, chopped
- Filé and hot sauce for the table (optional)

DIRECTIONS:

Make a dark roux with bacon grease or duck fat and the flour. When the roux has reached the right color, add the chopped onions and scallions. Stir well and allow the onions to begin to caramelize. Add celery and bell peppers. Add garlic. When the vegetables are all soft, add the sausage. After browning the sausage, add the leftover gravy. (Even if the gravy contains mushrooms and other vegetables, as mine does, add it all. Add stock or water to cover everything in the pot. Add the turkey carcass and leftover turkey cut into bite-sized pieces. Add bay leaves, thyme, cloves, and lemon. Simmer at least 2 hours so that the flavors can meld. Taste and adjust seasonings, especially salt and pepper. Add the chopped parsley. Remove the carcass before serving. Serve with cooked rice or Thanksgiving dressing.

LAKE CHARLES OXTAIL & GRITS

Chef Lyle Broussard,
Lake Charles, LA
Jack Daniels Bar & Grill at L'Auberg
Casino Resort

INGREDIENTS:

- 18 pounds oxtails
- 3 medium yellow onions, diced
- 4 garlic cloves, minced
- 3 pounds whole tomatoes (with juice)
- 6 quarts beef broth
- 6 ounces olive oil
- 4 green bell peppers, minced
- 4 ounces dark roux
- 5 celery stalks, minced

DIRECTIONS:

Season oxtails with salt and pepper. In a large cast iron pot, add oil and heat on medium heat. Place oxtails into heated oil and brown evenly on all sides. In the same braising pot, add onions, bell peppers, celery, and garlic. Season with salt and pepper. Cook until onions are tender and garlic has browned slightly. Add whole tomatoes and juice to the pot. Add beef broth. Cover pot and simmer for 2 hours and 15 minutes. After oxtails have become tender, remove from the pot and set aside. Stir in dark roux and let simmer for 5 minutes. After sauce has thickened, strain sauce, keeping only the thin liquid.

CRAWFISH ETOUFFEE (MAMOU STYLE)

Donna Reed Harper
New Orleans, LA, Dillard University
Assistant Registrar of Operations

INGREDIENTS:

- 12–16 ounces Louisiana frozen crawfish tails in bag with fat
- 1 stick butter
- ½ cup green bell peppers, chopped
- ½ cup celery, chopped
- ½ cup white onions, chopped
- 1 can cream of mushroom soup
- Water
- Season to taste

DIRECTIONS:

Cut a slit at the top of the crawfish tails bag and pour in a little water. Knead the tails to separate the fat from the tails. Pour out fat and water in a bowl to keep for later. You can repeat this to get all the fat off the tails. This will make up your gravy. Separate your tails and remove any debris left behind. Melt the butter in the pan you plan on using. Use a skillet with 3" depth. Add trio of vegetables and cook until tender. Add the soup to the water with crawfish fat and mix well. Slowly add the water and soup to skillet. Make sure to add a little at a time so the butter won't separate. Keep stirring until well blended. Season to taste. Simmer until you are almost ready to serve. Add the crawfish tails and heat for a few minutes. The tails are already cooked so you just need to heat them up. Pour over rice and make sure to have plenty of French bread to soak up the gravy.

AUNT LUCILLE'S STUFFED CRABS

Kemberley Washington
New Orleans, LA
Dillard University, Accounting Professor

INGREDIENTS:

- 2 cups of crab meat
- ½ cup of onion, finely chopped
- ½ cup of celery, finely chopped
- ½ cup of green bell pepper, finely chopped
- 2 garlic cloves, finely chopped
- ¾ cup of water
- ¾ cup of seasoned breadcrumbs
- 4 ounces of margarine (1 cube)
- 1 teaspoon of salt
- 1 teaspoon of cayenne pepper (optional)
- ¾ teaspoon of thyme
- 4 crab shells

DIRECTIONS:

Sauté onions, celery, green pepper, and garlic in 2 ounces (half) margarine. Add seasoning. Cook for 2 minutes; add water. Let cook for 5 minutes. Add crab meat and cook for 5 minutes. Add crumbs and let cook for 5 minutes. Remove from heat; add remaining margarine. Stuff crab shells or place contents in a greased casserole dish. Sprinkle crumbs on top. Bake for 20 minutes at 400 degrees.

GRANDMA ANNIE'S SMOTHERED OKRA & SHRIMP

Jon Renthrope
New Orleans, LA
Cajun Fire Brewing Company

INGREDIENTS:

- 3 pounds cut whole okra (fresh or frozen)
- 1–2 pounds of smoked sausage
- 3 pounds of fresh Louisiana shrimp (peeled and deveined)
- 1 white onion, chopped
- 1 bell pepper, chopped
- 3 cloves of garlic, chopped
- 3 stalks celery, chopped
- 1 teaspoon kosher salt
- 1 teaspoon cayenne pepper
- 2 tablespoons of Season-All
- 2 tablespoons vinegar
- 1 teaspoon extra virgin olive oil
- 1 cup seafood stock
- 1 bay leaf

DIRECTIONS:

Cook smoked sausage until fat is rendered, 6–8 minutes. Add garlic, bell pepper, yellow onion, and celery; sauté until golden, 10–12 minutes. Stir in remaining ingredients (chopped okra, ½ teaspoon of cayenne pepper, shrimp stock, and 2 tablespoons of vinegar); boil. Reduce heat to medium-low; cook covered, stirring occasionally (every 10 minutes), until okra is tender, 1–1 ½ hours. Add shrimp last 30 minutes of cooking. Allow dish to cool. Serve and enjoy.

For Seafood Stock: Be sure to save the shrimp shells, heads, and tails. Rinse with cold water. Add to 1 cup of water. Bring to boil. Add 1 bay leaf, 2 tablespoons of Season-All, ½ teaspoon of cayenne pepper. Simmer for 1 hour (until cooked down). Strain out shells and add to okra when recipe calls for addition.

"Okra is a staple and versatile ingredient of black communities throughout the South. For me growing up, sugarcane fields and long summer nights by the bayou were synonymous with warm bowls of the aromatic smothered seafood okra. My grandmother would routinely make this nutritious and savory recipe that I have continued to cook to this day."

The addition of vinegar helps break down the slime associated with cooked okra.

CREOLE JAMBALAYA

Ms. Sybil Haydel Morial
New Orleans, LA
Former First Lady of New Orleans

INGREDIENTS:

- ⅓ cup olive oil or vegetable oil
- 3 cups chopped onions
- 1 cup diced celery
- 1 cup diced bell peppers
  (green, red, and yellow combined)
- 3 cloves garlic, minced
- 1 pound andouille or smoked sausage
  (beef, turkey, or pork or combined)
- 1 ½ pounds cubed chicken (raw)
- 1 teaspoon cayenne pepper
- 1 large can diced tomatoes
- 1 medium can tomato sauce
- 2 cups chicken broth
- 3 bay leaves
- 3 cups rice (raw)
- 1 cup chopped green onions
- ½ cup chopped parsley

DIRECTIONS:

Heat oil and sauté seasonings until tender. Add sausage, stirring often, scrape the bottom of the pot to loosen browned particles. Brown chicken for 6 to 8 minutes, scraping the bottom of the pot (deglazing). Add garlic and stir. Add diced tomatoes, tomato sauce, and bay leaves. Stir in chicken broth. Taste for seasoning and add salt if needed. Add rice and stir for 2 to 3 minutes to coat evenly. Cook over medium heat covered for 30 to 35 minutes without stirring until rice is tender and the liquid has been absorbed. Add green onions and parsley. Remove from heat and let stand covered for 5 minutes. Remove bay leaves. If you include shrimp, add raw shrimp at the end and continue cooking until shrimp are pink (3–5 more minutes). To cook in the oven, pour mixture into a pan and bake uncovered in a pre-heated 350 degree oven for 35 minutes.

- -

MY MOTHER'S CREOLE WHITE BEANS

Ms. Sybil Haydel Morial
New Orleans, LA
Former First Lady of New Orleans

INGREDIENTS:

- 1 pound white beans,
  "White Northerns" preferred
- 1 large onion, chopped
- 5 cloves of garlic, minced
- 8 cups of chicken broth (canned is fine)
- 2 pounds smoked sausage
  (pork, beef, or turkey will do)
- 6 strips of bacon
- Black pepper to taste

DIRECTIONS:

Soak beans overnight in tap water to cover. In a large pot, put drained beans and chicken stock, bring to a boil, then reduce heat and cook for an hour until beans are soft. Stir occasionally. Mash some of the beans against the side of the pot with cooking spoon. This makes them creamy. While the beans are cooking, sauté bacon until done (do not cook to a crisp) and remove from pan. Sauté the onions lightly until translucent. Add minced garlic at the end (it burns easily). Set aside. Slice sausage and sauté in same pan to extract some of the oil. Add the seasonings and sausage to pot of beans and simmer for about half an hour over low heat. If they are a little stiff, add some water. Pour into a casserole dish and place bacon slices on top. Bake in a very low oven (275 degrees for about two hours). Salt is usually not needed because the chicken broth and sausage provide salt. Serve over rice. Add hot sauce to taste. They taste better the next day.

GRAN'S FILÈ GUMBO

Ms. Sybil Haydel Morial
New Orleans, LA
Former First Lady of New Orleans

INGREDIENTS:

- 3 cups of vegetable oil (not olive oil)
- 3 cups of flour
- 6 medium onions, chopped
- 4 ribs of celery, chopped
- 1 green bell pepper, chopped
- 1 red bell pepper, chopped
- 5 cloves of garlic, minced
- 4 stalks of green onions, chopped
- 1 tablespoon paprika
- 3 quarts of chicken stock or broth
- 4 dried bay leaves
- 1 tablespoon fresh thyme (or dried)
- 4 chicken breasts without skin
    or with skin during pre-cooking
- 4 chicken thighs without skin
    or with skin during pre-cooking
- 1 pound of andouille sausage,
    each slice about one half inch
- 1 pound of smoked sausage,
    each slice about one half inch
- ½ pound of hot sausage (optional)
- Filé

If you want to include seafood, add to the gumbo pot at the end:

- 2 pounds of raw, peeled, deveined shrimp
- 1 quart of oysters or 2 dozen

"Filè gumbo is a true Creole dish. It is truly unique and every family in New Orleans has their own recipe. My paternal grandmother, Gran, was an extraordinary cook. One of the secrets to a really good gumbo is the roux. You must constantly stir it over a medium low heat until it turns 'nut brown,' Gran's term. It may take 45 minutes so I usually make the roux the day before and complete the dish the day it is served.

DIRECTIONS:

The roux: Heat the oil in a heavy pot or pan. Put the heat on low and slowly add the flour while constantly stirring. You are cooking the flour. Do not stop stirring. It may take 40 minutes. When the roux is nut brown or milk chocolate brown, it is done. Remove the roux to a very big pot.

In a separate pan, sauté the seasonings (onions, celery bell peppers, green onions, and garlic) in a bit of vegetable oil until they are soft. Set aside. Sauté sliced andouille and smoked sausage in a bit of vegetable oil. Set aside. Sauté chicken until done, remove the skin and set aside. Put a bit of water in the pan to scrape the drippings to add to the pot later for more flavor.

Add the seasonings (garlic last because it burns easily) and herbs to the roux and on very low heat, stir for a few minutes. Add all the drippings to the pot and stir until blended. Then add the heated or room temperature chicken stock and simmer until it is very hot for about 5 minutes. Add the sausage and chicken bites to the pot and simmer on low heat until all ingredients are blended. Stir often.

Slowly add 1 cooking spoon full of filé while slowly stirring, about 2 minutes. Then, add another cooking spoonful of filé, slowly stirring. The filé thickens the gumbo. It should not be as thin as soup and not as thick as stew. You may need to add more filé until it is the right consistency. The pot continues to simmer on the lowest heat. If it is too thick, add a little more stock. If it is too thin, add a little more filé.

Now is the time to add seafood if you wish. Add the oysters to the simmering pot and when the edges curl, the oysters are done (about 3 minutes). Add a cup of oyster water to the pot. When the gumbo is hot, add the shrimp and cook until they turn pink. Turn off the heat and cover the pot. Serve over steamed rice.

QUEEN REESIE'S STUFFED MIRLITONS

Cherice Harrison-Nelson
New Orleans, LA
Mardi Gras Indian Maroon Queen, Guardians of the Flame

INGREDIENTS:

- 6 small or medium sized mirlitons
- 6 tablespoons of butter
- 1 cup of onion, diced
- 1 cup of green bell pepper, chopped
- 1 cup of celery, chopped
- ½ cup of green onions
- 2 garlic cloves, minced
- 1 pound of small to medium shrimp, peeled and deveined
- ½ pound of lump Louisiana crab meat
- 2–3 shakes of hot sauce
- Salt and pepper to taste
- 1 teaspoon of Chef Leon
- 1 cup of Reising stuffing mix
- ½ cup of Reising or Italian breadcrumbs
- 2 tablespoons of chopped fresh parsley

DIRECTIONS:

In a large pot of water, boil whole mirlitons until just tender to fork. Do not overcook. Cool, cut in half, remove and discard seeds and spoon out vegetable pulp, leaving shell thick enough to stuff, about ¼-inch thick. Coarsely chop mirliton pulp with fork. Place shells on a baking sheet and pulp in a colander. Cursively pick lump crab meat and remove shell pieces. Try not to break up lumps. Place on the side. Melt 4 tablespoons of the butter in a large, heavy skillet and sauté onions, bell pepper, and celery until transparent. Add garlic and sauté about 5 additional minutes. Watch carefully to not scorch garlic. Add shrimp, sauté until pink. Do not overcook. Add mirliton pulp, Chef Leon seasoning (Creole seasoning), salt, pepper, hot sauce, and cook on low heat, stirring until ingredients are thoroughly mixed, for about 1 minute. Remove from heat and add ¾–1 cup of the breadcrumbs and parsley. Mix well. Gently stir in crabmeat trying not to break up lumps. Divide stuffing equally into mirliton shells, sprinkle with breadcrumbs and dot with remaining 2 tablespoons of butter cut into ¼-inch cubes. To bake, place mirlitons on baking sheet and bake at 350 degrees until tops are browned and mirlitons are heated through, about 30 minutes. Stuffing mix can also be placed in a casserole dish and baked.

. . . .

SHRIMP STEW

Mrs. Sandra Peychaud Dalcour
New Orleans, LA
Wife of Mardi Gras Indian Big Chief Clarence Dalcour, Creole Osceolas

INGREDIENTS:

- 2 pounds of peeled medium size deveined shrimp
- 3 cloves of minced garlic
- 1 large onion, finely chopped
- 2 bay leaves
- Pinch of dried thyme
- 3 tablespoons of flour
- 1 stick of salted butter
- 3 cups of shrimp stock

DIRECTIONS:

Sauté butter, onions, garlic, thyme, and bay leaves in a skillet. Season with favorite seasoning. After onions are translucent, add 3 tablespoons of flour. Fry flour until golden brown. Add shrimp stock and cook down until thick. Add shrimp last. Do not overcook the shrimp. Serve with white cooked rice.

ROASTED PUMPKIN SOUP WITH CARDAMOM & CRÈME FRAICHE

*As featured in Charleston Magazine

Chef Kevin Mitchell
Charleston, SC
Culinary Institute of Charleston

INGREDIENTS:

- 1 9-pound pumpkin
  (9 cups of roasted pumpkin)
- 3 ½ tablespoons extra virgin olive oil
- 3 Fuji apples or 22 ounces
- 6 ounces shallots, minced
- 4 sprigs of thyme
- 1 quart plus
  ½ quart low sodium chicken broth
- Pinch of nutmeg
- Pinch of allspice
- 1 tablespoon of Kosher salt

PROSCIUTTO CRACKLINGS

- 3 ounces prosciutto

CARDAMOM CRÈME FRAICHE

- ½ cup crème fraiche
- ½ teaspoon ground cardamom

DIRECTIONS:

Preheat oven to 450 degrees. Wash pumpkin. Cut off top and scoop out seeds and remove innards from pumpkin. Cut into equal size wedges. Pierce flesh with a fork. Massage 1 ½ tablespoons oil into pumpkin. Place on baking sheet and roast in oven for 1 hour and 20 minutes. Wash, core, and chop apples. Peel shallots. Place apples and shallots on a separate baking sheet. Pour 1 tablespoon vegetable oil over apple slices and shallots. Add sprigs of thyme and roast in oven for one hour.

Remove pumpkin and apples from oven. Let cool. Once the pumpkin has cooled, scrape flesh from the skin. In a heavy bottomed soup pot, add 1 tablespoon vegetable oil and add roasted pumpkin, apples, and shallots. Sauté over medium heat for about 1 minute. Add chicken broth. Bring to a simmer over low heat for 10 minutes. In batches, puree mixture in blender and blend until smooth. Strain through fine mesh sieve. Pour back into soup pot. Add ½ quart chicken broth. Warm for 5 minutes. Adjust seasoning with salt. Stir in nutmeg and allspice. Pour soup into pre-warmed bowls. Finish with crème fraiche and prosciutto cracklings

For Cracklings: Preheat oven to 350 degrees. Line a baking sheet with parchment paper. Thinly slice prosciutto. Place prosciutto on prepared baking sheet. Bake for 15 minutes or until crisp. Cool. Crumble and hold for garnish

For Crème: Combine crème fraiche and ground cardamom. Mix until smooth.

SOUTHSIDE BEEF CHILI

Mrs. Bertha Glinsey
Chicago, IL
Homemaker, 84 years old

INGREDIENTS:

- 2 pounds of sirloin, cut into $\frac{1}{3}$-inch cubes
- 1 large onion, chopped
- 1 small green pepper, chopped
- 4 garlic cloves, minced
- 2 to 3 tablespoons of chili powder
- 1 ½ teaspoons of ground cumin
- 1 teaspoon of dried oregano, crushed
- ¼ teaspoon dried coriander, crushed
- 2 tablespoons of olive oil
- 1 can of plum tomatoes (28 ounces) undrained and chopped
- 1 can of tomato sauce (13 ounces)
- 1 cup of beef broth
- 1 tablespoon of packed brown sugar
- Dash of crushed red pepper
- 2 cans of chili beans
- Salt and pepper to taste

DIRECTIONS:

In a Dutch oven cook and stir beef, onion, green pepper, garlic, chili powder, cumin, oregano, and coriander until meat is brown. Add remaining ingredients except beans. Heat to boiling. Reduce heat, cover, and simmer for about 1 hour. Stir in chili beans; continue to cook uncovered for 30 minutes.

CHARLESTON OKRA SOUP (THE REAL O.G. GUMBO)

Chef Benjamin Dennis
Charleston, SC

INGREDIENTS:

- 5 ripe tomatoes, chopped
- 2–3 cloves of garlic, finely minced
- 1 teaspoon fresh ginger, minced
- 1 small onion, diced
- 1 bay leaf
- 3 sprigs of thyme
- 2 teaspoons fresh chili pepper, minced or dried
- 2 ears of corn, cut into thirds
- 2 cups fresh butter beans or field peas
- 5 cups okra, sliced ½-inch thick
- ½ pound favorite smoked meat, cooked and broth reserved (optional) or just water

DIRECTIONS:

Add a little oil to a small stew pot. Enough to cover bottom of the pan. Add tomato and stir constantly over high heat for 5 minutes. Season the tomatoes. Add your herbs and spices, cook for another minute. Then add your stock or water and beans. Bring to a simmer and cook until peas are almost tender. Add okra, corn, and smoked meat (if using) and cook until okra is tender, 5 to 10 minutes, depends on the okra. Check seasoning and serve with rice. This recipe is the base for so many different things. Add shrimp, crab, poultry, or just keep it vegan.

· ·

SAUTEED SHRIMP CAKES WITH HERB MUSTARD SAUCE

Chef Joseph G. Randall
Savannah, GA
Chef Joe Randall's Cooking School

INGREDIENTS:

- 2 pounds of jumbo fresh shrimp (peeled and deveined)
- 2 egg whites
- ¼ cup of mayonnaise
- 1 tablespoon of fresh dill, chopped
- ½ teaspoon of dry mustard
- 1 teaspoon of fresh lemon juice
- 3 cups of fresh breadcrumbs
- 1 cup of peanut oil
- Salt and pepper to taste

DIRECTIONS:

Peel and devein the shrimp and remove the tails. Place half of the shrimp meat in a food processor fitted with a metal blade. Puree smooth for 1 to 2 minutes. Add the egg whites and puree for 1 minute longer. Pour the mixture into a large bowl and stir in the mayonnaise, dill, mustard, lemon juice, salt, and pepper to taste. Mix well. Chop the remaining shrimp coarsely and add to the mixture. Form into six cakes (each about 3 ½ ounces) about 1-inch thick. Coat each cake with fresh breadcrumbs. Heat the oil in a cast iron skillet over medium high heat. Fry the shrimp cakes 3 to 4 minutes on both sides or until golden brown. Drain on paper towels. Keep the cakes warm in a pre-heated 200 degree oven.

SLOWCOOKED SOUTHERN BUTTERBEANS & OKRA

Dr. Howard Jason Conyers
New Orleans, LA (originally from Manning, SC)
NASA Rocket Scientist and
South Carolina Whole Hog Preservationist

INGREDIENTS:

- 2 pounds of fresh butter beans
  or frozen lima beans (not dried)
- ½ pound of fresh field peas (not dried)
- 2 cups of fresh okra, chopped
- 2 teaspoons of salt for starter
- 1 teaspoon of black pepper
- 1 tablespoon of sugar
- 2 smoked ham hocks

"During the summer, I would visit my grandmother's house in Nichols, South Carolina, and we would shell peas and beans in a porcelain wash tub after a few bushels were freshly picked. After a while the shelling of peas and beans would make the area under your fingernail tender and sore. The discomfort caused by shelling was forgotten the next day after you had this dish with a nice pot of rice."

DIRECTIONS:

First cook ham hocks overnight in slow cooker until tender, remove from juice, and cool juice by sitting in refrigerator so the grease will rise to the top and the juice will be at the bottom. Remove ends from okra and bake in oven for 30 minutes at 375 degrees. Place 2 pounds of fresh butter beans and peas in crock pot and fill with water until only about 1" of beans are exposed, as the beans will release water as well. Take a cup of gelatin (juice) from cooked ham hocks and placed into crock pot. Add baked okra, black pepper, sugar, and salt to taste last, as the smoked ham hocks can make the dish unusually salty. Cook in pot on low heat on stove until tender or place in a crock pot for about 6 hours until the beans are soft. This vegetable dish is always served with a dry pot of rice.

HOPPIN JOHN

Audrey Vice
Moncks Corner, SC

INGREDIENTS:

- 2 cups of dry cowpeas
- 2 cups of parboiled rice
- 1 smoked ham hock or pork neckbone
- Dash of crushed red pepper
- Salt and pepper
- 8 ½ cups of water
- 4 slices of salt pork or slices of bacon
  (or substitute with 3 tablespoons of oil)

DIRECTIONS:

Rinse ham hock or neckbone well with warm water. Place in a medium pot with 2–2 ½ cups of water. Cover and cook on medium for approximately 30 minutes or until the water has boiled off. Leave the ham hock or neckbone in the pot and set aside. In separate pot/skillet, cook the slices of salt pork or bacon until mostly cooked on both sides or slightly browned.

Rinse cowpeas thoroughly with water and drain. In the medium pot with the cooked ham hock or neckbone, add cowpeas, the additional cooked meats, 6 cups of fresh water, and crushed red pepper. Bring to a boil, cover, and simmer for about 1 hour or until peas are tender. Optional: after peas are tender, remove meats from pot.

Add 2 cups of raw rice to the peas and liquid in the pot. Liquid and peas together should equate to 4 cups. If no bacon or salt pork was used, add 3 tablespoons of oil. Season with salt and pepper, only if needed, to taste. Bring to a boil and cover. Reduce heat to simmer for about 20–25 minutes or per the directions provided for cooking the rice, stirring occasionally. If meats were removed from peas, chop meats and remove from the bones while the rice is cooking. After 20–25 minutes, remove the lid (add chopped meat), stir with fork, and serve.

KOSHARY (EGYPT)
The most famous Egyptian dish in Egypt

Dr. Abdullah Darwish
New Orleans, LA, Dillard University
Professor and Chair of Physics and
Pre-Engineering Department

INGREDIENTS:

- 1 can chickpeas (14.5 ounces), drained and rinsed
- ¼ cup white vinegar
- 1 teaspoon ground coriander
- 1 teaspoon ground cayenne pepper
- ½ teaspoon ground cumin
- ½ (16 ounces) package ditalini pasta
- 1 ½ cups short-grain rice, rinsed cold water
- 1 ½ cups dark brown lentils
- 1 pinch of salt and ground black pepper to taste
- 1 tablespoon olive oil
- 2 yellow onions, minced
- 4 cloves garlic, minced
- 1 can crushed tomatoes (14 ounces)
- 2 tablespoons butter
- 3 cups of hot water for the rice

DIRECTIONS:

Combine the chickpeas, vinegar, cayenne pepper, and cumin in container with a tight-fitting lid. Store in refrigerator while prepping remainder of dish, shaking occasionally. Bring a pot of lightly salted water to a rolling boil. Cook the ditalani pasta in the boiling water until cooked through but firm to the bite, about 8 minutes; drain and set aside. Combine the rice with enough cold water to cover; allow to soak for 15 minutes. Drain. Meanwhile, combine the lentils with enough water to cover in a pot; season with salt and pepper. Bring the lentils to a boil and cook at a boil until tender, about 25 minutes. Drain. Heat the olive oil in a saucepan over medium-high heat; cook and stir the onion and garlic in the hot oil until translucent, 5 to 7 minutes. Add the crushed tomatoes, season with salt and pepper, reduce heat to medium-low, and maintain at a simmer while preparing remainder of dish. Melt the butter in a pot over medium-high heat. Add the rice to the butter, increase heat to high, and fry for 4 to 5 minutes, stirring constantly. Pour 3 cups of hot water over the rice; bring to a boil. Season the rice mixture with salt and pepper, reduce heat to low, cover the pot, and cook until rice is tender and the liquid has been absorbed, about 20 minutes. Caramelize about 4 large onions in butter and brown sugar for about 45 minutes at the same time you are cooking the rice.

Mix the rice and lentils together on a large serving platter. Spread the cooked ditalani over the rice and lentil mixture. Serve with the marinated chickpeas, the tomato sauce, and the caramelized onion over the top of the plate.

BLACK-EYED PEAS HUMMUS
WITH WEST AFRICAN CHILI PASTE

Chef Pierre Thiam
New York, NY via Dakar, Senegal

INGREDIENTS:

CHILE PASTE

- ¼ cup plus 2 tablespoons
  red palm oil or vegetable oil
- ¼ cup crushed red chile flakes
- 2 tablespoons tomato paste
- 2 tablespoons dried crawfish
- 2 tablespoons fermented fish powder
- 2 tablespoons smoked dried shrimp
- 1 tablespoon chipotle chile powder
  or smoked paprika
- 1 teaspoon onion powder
- 1 teaspoon minced garlic
- 1 teaspoon minced ginger
- ½ medium yellow onion,
  roughly chopped

HUMMUS

- 2 red bell peppers
- 2 cups dried black-eyed peas,
  soaked overnight, drained
- ½ cup fresh lemon juice
- 2 tablespoons red palm
  oil or vegetable oil
- 2 teaspoons minced ginger
- 1 teaspoon of cayenne
- 2 cloves garlic, minced
- Kosher salt and
  freshly ground black pepper
- Flatbread or crudité, for serving

DIRECTIONS:

Make the chile paste in a small food processor, combine 2 tablespoons palm oil with the chile flakes, tomato paste, crawfish, fish powder, shrimp, chile powder, onion powder, garlic, ginger, and onion and purée until smooth. In a small saucepan, heat the remaining ¼ cup palm oil over medium-low. Scrape the chile purée into the pan and cook, stirring occasionally until it turns dark brown and caramelized, about 30 minutes. Transfer the paste to a jar and refrigerate until ready to use, preferably at least 8 hours. Make the hummus: Heat the broiler. Place the bell peppers on a baking sheet and broil, turning as needed, until charred all over, about 15 minutes. Transfer the peppers to a bowl, cover with plastic wrap, and let stand for 15 minutes to steam. Uncover the peppers and remove and discard their skins, stems, and seeds. Finely chop the pepper flesh and transfer to bowl.

In a 4-quart saucepan, cover the peas with 3 cups water and bring to a boil. Reduce the heat to maintain a steady simmer and cook, stirring, until the peas are very tender, 12 to 15 minutes. Remove the peas from the heat and let cool for 10 minutes. Drain the peas and reserve 1 ½ cups of the cooking liquid. Pour the reserved cooking liquid into a food processor along with the lemon juice, palm oil, ginger, cayenne, and garlic and purée for 20 seconds to blend flavors. Add the cooked peas, season liberally with salt and pepper, and purée until very smooth. Scrape the purée into a serving bowl and top with the roasted peppers. Serve with flatbreads or crudité and the chile paste on the side.

> "In this nod to hummus, I use black-eyed peas, which to me symbolizes the food that captive Africans brought to the Americas. In my native Senegal, the black-eyed pea is a common staple used in making fritters (akara), stews (Ndambe), or a rice dish very similar to Hoppin' Johns (Tiébou Niébé). Here, the cooked peas are puréed with lemon juice, ginger, and spices; and served with an intensely aromatic Ghanaian chili paste (Shito). The paste will last for a month in the refrigerator. You can substitute the chili paste with your favorite chili sauce, if you like."

COWPEAS (MPINDI/KUNDE)

Edie Mukiibi
Kampala, Uganda
Vice-President, Slow Food International

INGREDIENTS:

- 2 pounds cow peas (fresh or dried)
- 2 tomatoes, diced
- 1 yellow onion, chopped
- ½ green bell pepper, minced
- ½ teaspoon salt
- 5 cups of water
- ½ cup of cooking oil
- ½ teaspoon curry powder

DIRECTIONS:

In a pan, bring the cowpeas to boil until tender. In another saucepan, fry the onions, add the green pepper, cover, and let it simmer for a few minutes before adding tomatoes. Let it simmer for several minutes after adding tomatoes. Mash the cow peas a little bit to create a paste-like thick solution. Add the cowpeas without water and let it simmer for a few minutes before adding the curry powder and other spices. Add the remaining water and let simmer. Serve with steamed bananas, cassava, or sweet potatoes.

 Cowpeas are a multipurpose legume crop that can thrive under semi-arid conditions prevalent in Uganda. They are known as "obushaza" in Runyankole, Mpindi in Luganda, and Kunde in Swahili. The crops' rapid maturation over the years have helped African families survive the hungry season between cereal harvests. They are also dried and kept for a very long time without being affected by weevils. The leaves are also steamed, solar dried, and mashed to form a powder called "eggobe" that is kept for long and used to season meat and other foods.

JOLLOF RICE

Chef Tunde Wey
New Orleans, LA (Originally from Lagos and Detroit)

INGREDIENTS:

- 2 ripe tomatoes, chopped
- 1 onion, minced
- 1 green bell pepper, chopped
- 6 cups of long grain parboiled rice
- Vegetable oil
- 2 scotch bonnet peppers
- 3 tablespoons of curry powder
- 1 tablespoon of black pepper
- 1 ½ tablespoons of garlic powder
- 2 tablespoons of onion powder
- 1 tablespoon of ginger powder
- 2 tablespoons of dry thyme
- 2 tablespoons of Maggi

DIRECTIONS:

Wash vegetables. Blend tomatoes, scotch bonnet, onions, and bell peppers (remove seeds from bell peppers). Heat vegetable oil. Add blended vegetables into hot oil, medium-high heat and bring to a boil. Add maggi and powdered spices; curry, pepper, garlic, ginger, thyme, nutmeg, and onion and lower to medium heat. Add rice, stir frequently to avoid burning. Cook until stew is soaked up by the rice and rice is soft.

DARLENE DELICIOUS CURRY CHICKEN

Darlene A. Moore
Pastor, Winan United Methodist Church
Class of 1986, Dillard University

INGREDIENTS:

- 3 to 5 pounds of chicken wings
- 2 bay leaves
- 1 small chopped onion
- ½ teaspoon of soul seasoning
- Garlic powder (optional)
- 1 minced garlic clove
- ½ cup of chopped green bell pepper
- 1 chopped celery stalk
- Margarine/butter to taste
- 1 teaspoon of yellow mustard
- Dash of Louisiana hot sauce
- 1 can of chicken gravy
- 1 to 3 teaspoons of ready made roux
- ⅓ cup of dried parsley flakes
- 1 ½ teaspoons of curry powder
- 1 seeded and minced jalapeño pepper
- 1 ½ cups of chicken drippings
    or chicken broth

Fried Plantains
- 3 green plantains, sliced into chips
- Vegetable or canola oil
- Slap Ya Mama seasoning

DIRECTIONS:

Heat oven to 400 degrees. Wash chicken, then season with favorite soul seasoning, mustard, and garlic powder. Marinate for at least two hours. Sauté chopped celery, green bell pepper, onion, and garlic with margarine/butter in large frying pan on low-medium heat. Add seasoning. Cook for 8 minutes or until vegetables are softened. Set aside and place on a separate plate.

Place seasoned chicken wings in a baking pan and add inch of water. Cook wings for 25 minutes in the oven then turn over and cook for 10 more minutes. Take a large frying pan and add one small can of chicken gravy, 1 ½ cups of chicken drippings or chicken broth on medium heat. Add and stir in smooth brown gravy roux and ½ teaspoon of more curry powder. Add already baked chicken to the pan along with bay leaves, hot sauce, sautéed seasoning, and more soul seasoning to taste. Cover and cook for 15 more minutes at low-medium heat. Serve over white or brown rice. Serves 4.

For Fried Plantains: Peel and slice green plantains. Heat oil in a deep frying pan at medium-high heat. Fry plantains until golden brown and remove from frying pan. Place fried plantains on a plate with thick paper towels. Season with Slap Ya Mama seasoning. Serve with curry chicken and rice. Serves 4.

DORO WAT
(ETHIOPIAN CHICKEN)

Dr. Wodajo Welldaregay
New Orleans, LA, Dillard University
Chair and Associate Professor of Public Health

INGREDIENTS:

- 2 pounds of chicken legs, unskinned
- 2 lemons, squeezed
- 2 large red onions, finely minced
- ½ cup of garlic, finely minced
- ½ cup of fresh ginger, finely minced
- 6 peeled hard-boiled eggs
- 2 cups of Berbere seasoning
- 1 cup of Niter Kibbeh
    (Ethiopian Spiced Butter)
- Salt

Berbere seasoning:
- ½ teaspoon of fenugreek
- 1 teaspoon of ground ginger
- 1 teaspoon of onion powder
- ½ teaspoon of ground cardamom
- ½ cup of chili powder
- 1 teaspoon of dried basil
- 1 teaspoon of black and white pepper
- ¼ cup of smoked paprika
- 1 tablespoon of salt

Niter Kibbeh:
- 6 pounds of salted butter
- ⅓ cup of dried thyme
- ⅓ cup of dried oregano
- ⅓ cup of cardamom seeds
- ⅓ cup of black cumin

DIRECTIONS:

Make the Ethiopian butter and Niter Kibbeh the night before in a food processor. Cover and refrigerate. Ground spices in a food processor. Set aside. Remove skin from chicken legs. Rinse and marinate in cold water and squeezed lemon in a bowl.

In a large pot, caramelize the red onions on low heat for 1 hour. Add the berbere seasoning, Niter Kibbeh butter, minced garlic, and ginger and cook for 30 minutes on medium-low heat. Add the marinated chicken and cook on medium-low heat, 30 to 45 minutes. Add in the hard-boiled eggs and salt to taste. Simmer on low heat for fifteen minutes and serve on Ethiopian Injera bread.

KOLKATA INDIA
VEGETABLE CROQUETTES

Dr. Julie Basu-Ray
New Orleans, LA, Dillard University
Assistant Professor of Biology

INGREDIENTS:

- 2 medium red beets
- 1 large carrot, minced
- 3 medium cooked potatoes, skinned and mashed
- Vegetable oil
- 2 tablespoons of ginger, grated
- 1 medium onion, minced
- 3–4 green chillies, chopped in rounds
- 1 teaspoon of whole coriander seeds
- 1 teaspoon of cumin
- 1 teaspoon of dried chillies
- 1 teaspoon of ground cardamom
- 1 bay leaf
- 1 cinnamon stick
- Pinch of sugar
- Salt to taste
- ½ cup of peanuts or other nut (optional)
- 1 tablespoon of cilantro, chopped finely
- ¼ cup of raisins (optional)
- Plain breadcrumbs
- 2 eggs, eggwash

DIRECTIONS:

Remove skin from potatoes and beets. Boil 3 medium size potatoes until fork tender. Add beets and carrot to the pot when the potatoes are semi-fork tender. Bring vegetable mixture to a boil until fork tender. Do not overcook. Drain water and mash vegetables. The texture can be a little chunky. In a pan, lightly roast peanuts. Remove and set aside. In the same pan, lightly toast coriander seeds, cumin, dried chillies, then grind them to a powder. Add 1 teaspoon of ground cardamom, bay leaf, cinnamon stick, salt to taste, and a pinch of sugar. Grind spice blend. Set aside.

In a saucepan, heat oil on medium heat. Add 2 tablespoons of grated ginger, chopped onions, and green chillies. Add the mashed vegetables and 3 teaspoons of the ground spice blend. Sauté the mashed vegetables, mixing with spices until the excess water dries up and the vegetables come together. Add roasted peanuts. Turn off the heat and let the vegetable mixture cool.

When the mixture cools, grease your palms and form croquettes with them. You can add raisins to each. The usual shape is oblong or oval. Cover in a bowl and refrigerate overnight. Coat the croquettes with egg wash and plain breadcrumbs. In a pan heat oil for deep frying. Fry until golden brown and serve with tomato ketchup and mustard.

CUBAN CHICKEN SOUP

Zella Palmer
New Orleans, LA
Chair, Dillard University Ray Charles Program

INGREDIENTS:

- 3 pounds of chicken thighs
- 3 garlic cloves, minced
- 1 can of tomato paste
- 1 pound of eddoe, peeled and chopped
- 2 malanga, peeled and chopped
- 1 small pumpkin, seeded and chopped
- 1 tablespoon of cumin
- 1 teaspoon of Adobo seasoning
- 1 teaspoon of salt
- 1 teaspoon of white pepper
- 1 package of soup noodles
- Lime wedges
- Cooking oil
- 1 quart of water

DIRECTIONS:

Wash and remove skin from chicken thighs. Season chicken with cumin, pepper, salt, and Adobo. In a large stock pot, heat cooking oil on medium-low heat. Add chicken and brown. Add chopped garlic, constantly stirring so it coats the chicken. Add tomato paste. Continue to stir. Add water and bring to a boil. Remove skin and chop in large chunks the eddoe, malanga, and pumpkin. Remove chicken thighs from the water. Keep chicken stock. Remove bones from the cooked chicken thighs and chop chicken in chunks. Return the chicken to the pot, add the eddoe and malanga, and cook in stock until fork tender. Add pumpkin and ½ a packet of soup noodles. Cook for another 10 minutes or until the noodles are soft. Serve soup with lime wedges.

 Eddoe, malanga, and pumpkin can be bought at any Caribbean, African, or Latino grocery store.

PUERTO RICAN CREOLE LASAGNA

Zella Palmer
New Orleans, LA
Chair, Dillard University Ray Charles Program

INGREDIENTS:

- 2 pounds of ground meat (beef)
- 10 ripe black plantains
- 2 cans of tomato sauce (8 ounces)
- 1 ½ cups of grated cheese
- 1 pint of sour cream
- Salt and pepper to taste
- 1 medium onion, minced
- 1 garlic clove, minced
- 1 green bell pepper, minced

DIRECTIONS:

Preheat oven to 350 degrees. Season ground beef. Add onion, bell pepper, and garlic clove to meat. Mix well with hands. In a pan, brown ground beef; drain oil. In a pot, add ground meat mixture and 2 cans of tomato sauce. Bring to a low boil. Season to taste. Peel ripe black plantains and cut in large chunks on a slant. Fry plantains until light golden brown. Drain oil from plantains on a thick paper towel. In a deep baking dish, assemble the lasagna. Add 1 cup of the ripe cooked plantains to the bottom of the pan and smash with a flat spoon. The plantains are the lasagna noodles. The plantain layer should be about ½-inch thick. For the next layer, add meat mixture. Dollop sour cream over meat mixture lightly. Add a layer of grated cheese. Add the next layer of plantains and repeat previous steps. Cook for 35 minutes at 350 degrees.

TUSCAN WHITE BEAN SOUP

Donna Cummings
New Orleans, LA
Co-founder, Whitney Plantation

INGREDIENTS:

- Chicken broth, 4 cups
- 3 large Italian sausage links (two mild and 1 hot)
- 3 cans of dried beans
- 3–4 large carrots, chopped
- 1 large yellow onion, minced
- 1 bunch of fresh kale, chopped
- Tony Chachere's Creole seasoning
- Fresh ground black pepper
- ¼ cup of Italian grated cheese

DIRECTIONS:

Into a soup pot on a medium fire, add a cup of chicken broth. (The soup is best if the broth is homemade from leftover chicken bones, but store-bought will work.) Remove the sausage meat from the casing and put it into the boiling broth, breaking it up into small pieces with a wooden spoon as it cooks. Peel and chop the onion, clean and chop the carrots, and put the chopped onion and carrots on top of the (now cooked) sausage. Drain the cans of beans, rinse with water, and add the beans to the pot with enough of the remaining chicken broth to cover everything. Add the Creole seasoning and pepper to suit your taste. (If you used at least one link of hot Italian sausage, you will need less seasoning!) Stir the soup and let it come back to a medium boil. As soon as it reaches a boil, stir it again, turn the heat down to low, and put the lid on the pot. Let it cook for about two hours, stirring occasionally to make sure it doesn't stick to the bottom and burn, and add broth as necessary.

Just before serving, wash and clean about 6 big leaves of the kale (remove the tough rib from each leaf). Chop the kale into small pieces and add the chopped leaves to the soup, stirring the kale into the soup. Let the kale cook about five minutes and turn the soup off. Put the soup into warmed bowls and garnish with grated Italian cheese on top (parmesan or romano).

If you plan on making enough to freeze some for another meal, take that part out of the pot and freeze it before you add the kale and put fresh kale in when you warm it up. The kale always looks bright green and still has some crunch when you serve the soup.

MEXICAN CRAWFISH CORNBREAD

Dr. Yolanda W. Page
New Orleans, LA, Dillard University
Vice-President, Academic Affairs

INGREDIENTS:

- 1 ½ boxes Jiffy mix
- 2 eggs
- ¼ cup oil
- 1 tablespoon salt
- 1 teaspoon baking soda
- 1 medium onion, finely chopped
- 1 pound crawfish
- 1 jalapeño, finely chopped
- 1 cup shredded cheddar cheese
- 1 can cream-style corn
- Seasoning to taste.

DIRECTIONS: Combine all ingredients; bake in ungreased deep pan at 350 degrees for 30 minutes.

OVEN ROASTED OKRA

Chef Gason Nelson
New Orleans, LA

INGREDIENTS:

- 1 pound okra, rinsed and dried
- ½ tablespoon olive oil
- Zest of 1 lemon
- 2 teaspoons fresh thyme
- ¼ teaspoon onion powder
- ¼ teaspoon garlic powder
- Kosher salt and pepper to taste
- Pinch of cayenne pepper

DIRECTIONS:

Preheat oven to 450. Trim the okra by cutting away the stem ends and the tips, just the very ends. Then cut the okra in half, lengthwise. Place okra in a large bowl. Add oil, zest of the lemon, and spices and stir to coat the okra halves. Place okra on a baking sheet in a single layer. Roast in the oven for 20–25 minutes, shaking the okra at least twice during the roasting time. You'll know the okra is ready when it's lightly browned and tender. Serve hot—they tend to lose the crispy texture as they cool.

• •

CORNBREAD WITH CHEESE AND CHILES
Makes 8 servings

Toni Tipton-Martin, Austin, TX
Author of *The Jemima Code: Two Centuries of African American Cookbooks* and Co-Founder, Southern Foodways Alliance

INGREDIENTS:

- 2 cups yellow cornmeal
- 1 tablespoon sugar
- 1 teaspoon baking powder
- ½ teaspoon baking soda
- ½ teaspoon salt
- ½ cup shortening
- ¾ to 1 cup buttermilk
- 1 egg, beaten
- 1 can cream-style corn (14.75 ounces)
- 1 can diced green chiles (4 ounces)
- ¼ cup chopped green onion
- 1 cup shredded cheddar cheese

DIRECTIONS:

In a large mixing bowl, combine cornmeal, sugar, baking powder, soda, and salt. Mix well with a wire whisk. Melt the shortening in an 8-inch cast iron skillet. Pour shortening, buttermilk, and beaten egg into the dry ingredients and mix with a wooden spoon until just moist. Stir in the corn, chiles, and green onion and pour half the batter into the hot skillet. Sprinkle with cheese. Top with remaining batter. Bake in a preheated 375 degree oven 40 minutes or until done.

BLACK BEAN AND SPINACH ENCHILADAS

M. Shannon Williamson, M.S.
New Orleans, LA, Dillard University
Assistant Director, Academic Center for Excellence

INGREDIENTS:

ENCHILADAS:

- 1 tablespoon of olive oil
- 15-ounce can of rinsed and drained black beans
- 1 ½ cups of frozen or canned corn
- 8 ounces of fresh spinach
- 6 green onions, chopped
- ⅓ cup of cilantro, chopped
- 1 teaspoon of cumin
- 1 ½ cups of shredded cheddar cheese
- 8–10 large corn or wheat tortillas

ENCHILADA SAUCE:

- 1 teaspoon of butter
- 2 garlic cloves, minced
- 1 cup of vegetable stock
- 2 teaspoons of cumin
- ¼ teaspoon of salt
- ¼ teaspoon of pepper
- 1 cup of salsa verde
- ½ cup of Greek yogurt
- ¼ cup of cilantro, chopped
- 1 teaspoon of butter

DIRECTIONS:

Preheat oven to 375 degrees. To make the sauce, begin by making a roux. Heat butter over medium heat in a small saucepan. Add garlic and stir until fragrant, about 1 minute. Add flour and whisk for 2 minutes. Add vegetable stock and whisk until well combined and the mixture begins to simmer and thicken up. Add cumin, salt, and pepper. Take the saucepan off of the heat and stir in salsa verde, Greek yogurt, and cilantro. Set aside.

Next, make the enchilada filling. Heat a skillet over medium heat. Add olive oil and spinach, tossing until the spinach is just wilted. In a mixing bowl, add black beans, corn, sauteed spinach, green onion, cilantro, and cumin; stir to combine. Add ½ cup cheese, mixing until well incorporated.

In the bottom of a greased casserole dish, ladle 1 cup of enchilada sauce in the bottom. To assemble the enchiladas, take a tortilla, add a spoon of sauce and about ½ cup of enchilada filling in a tortilla, roll it up and place in the casserole dish. Repeat until all of the filling has been used. Make sure the enchiladas are packed tightly to prevent them from falling apart when baked.

Top with remaining enchilada sauce and 1 cup of cheese. Bake for 20 minutes until the cheese is bubbly and slightly golden brown. Remove from the oven and let cool for 10 minutes. Garnish with leftover cilantro and enjoy!

You can add 2 cups of shredded chicken to the enchilada filling to please the meat lovers in your family. Or, get creative and make ½ and ½ by adding 1 cup of shredded chicken to half of the filling.

ROASTED ALMONDS with MAPLE SYRUP + CAYENNE PEPPER

Julia Turshen
Accord, NY, Author of *Small Victories*,
Feed the Resistance, and *Now & Again*

INGREDIENTS:

- 1 tablespoon extra-virgin olive oil
- 2 tablespoons maple syrup
- ½ teaspoon kosher salt
- ½ teaspoon cayenne pepper
- 2 cups whole raw almonds

DIRECTIONS:

Preheat the oven to 350 degrees. Line a sheet pan with parchment paper and set it aside.

In a large bowl, whisk together the olive oil, maple syrup, salt, and cayenne. Add the almonds and stir everything together so that each and every almond is coated with the maple mixture. Transfer the nuts to the prepared sheet pan and spread them out so that they're in an even layer. Roast, stirring once or twice while they're in the oven until the nuts are browned and smell very toasty, 20 minutes. Remove the sheet pan from the oven and allow the nuts to cool completely (they will crisp as they cool). Serve at room temperature. Makes 2 cups

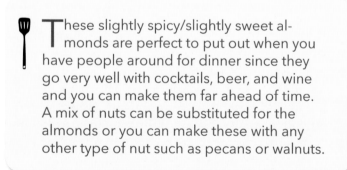

These slightly spicy/slightly sweet almonds are perfect to put out when you have people around for dinner since they go very well with cocktails, beer, and wine and you can make them far ahead of time. A mix of nuts can be substituted for the almonds or you can make these with any other type of nut such as pecans or walnuts.

OREO CHEESECAKE

Mrs. Adria N. Kimbrough, Esq.
New Orleans, LA, Dillard University First Lady
and Pre-Law Advisor,
Center for Law and Public Interest

INGREDIENTS:

Crust:
- 4 tablespoons butter, melted
- 18 Oreo cookies, crushed fine

Filling:
- 3 pounds cream cheese, at room temperature
- 2 ¾ cups granulated sugar
- 5 eggs
- 2 teaspoons pure vanilla extract
- 15 Oreo cookies, broken into chunks

Garnish:
- 12 ounces whipped cream
  (can use canned whipped cream)
- 12 Oreo cookies

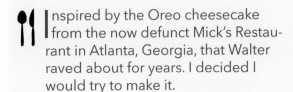

Inspired by the Oreo cheesecake from the now defunct Mick's Restaurant in Atlanta, Georgia, that Walter raved about for years. I decided I would try to make it.

DIRECTIONS:

For Crust: Heat oven to 250 degrees. Wrap outside of 10-inch springform pan tightly with foil (to prevent water from leaking in). Line bottom with a parchment circle. Set aside. In medium bowl, stir together butter and Oreo crumbs. Place in pan and press down firmly and evenly. Bake for 8–10 minutes. Remove from oven; set aside to cool.

For Filling: Place cream cheese in mixing bowl and mix on medium speed until soft (6–8 minutes). Use rubber spatula to scrape bowl often to ensure even distribution. Add sugar and blend well, scraping bowl just until smooth (no lumps). Reduce mixing speed to low, then slowly add eggs and vanilla. Mix until combined. Remove from mixer. Stir Oreo chunks into batter. Pour into pan. Place cheesecake pan into large roasting pan. Fill pan with water, leaving 1 inch of space from top of cheesecake pan. (Note: If you can't make the water bath work, place the large roasting pan of water on the rack directly underneath the cheesecake for a similar effect.)

Bake in a preheated oven for 2 ½ hours, until top of cheesecake is slightly golden. Let rest at room temperature for 1 ½ hours. Refrigerate at least 24 hours before serving. For garnish top each slice of cheesecake with 1 ounce of real whipped cream and an Oreo cookie.

QUICK ITALIAN CREAM CAKE

Mrs. Adria N. Kimbrough, Esq.
New Orleans, LA, Dillard University First Lady
and Pre-Law Advisor,
Center for Law and Public Interest

INGREDIENTS:

- White cake mix with pudding
- 3 eggs
- 1 ¼ cups buttermilk
- ¼ cup vegetable oil
- 1 (3 ½-ounce) can flaked coconut (optional)
- ⅔ cup chopped pecans, toasted

Cream Cheese Frosting:

- 1 ½ packages (12 ounces)
  cream cheese, softened
- ¾ cup butter or margarine, softened
- 6 cups powdered sugar
- 1 cup chopped pecans, toasted
- 2 teaspoons vanilla extract
- Garnish: pecan halves

DIRECTIONS:

Beat first 4 ingredients at medium speed with an electric mixer 2 minutes. Stir in coconut and pecans. Pour batter into 3 greased and floured 9" round cake pans. Bake at 350 degrees for 15 to 17 minutes or until a wooden toothpick inserted in center comes out clean. Cool in pans on wire racks 10 minutes. Remove from pans and cool completely on wire racks. Sprinkle cake layers evenly with rum, if desired; let stand 10 minutes.

For Cream Cheese Frosting: Beat cream cheese and butter at medium speed with an electric mixer until smooth. Gradually add powdered sugar, beating until light and fluffy. Stir in pecans and vanilla. Makes 4 cups. Spread Cream Cheese Frosting between layers and on top and sides of cake. Garnish, if desired. Chill 2 hours before slicing.

OATMEAL CHOCOLATE CHIP COOKIES

Mrs. Marjorie L. Kimbrough
Atlanta, GA

INGREDIENTS:

- ½ cup butter
- ½ cup Crisco
- 1 cup granulated sugar
- 1 cup light brown sugar
- 2 eggs
- 1 teaspoon vanilla extract
- 2 cups all-purpose flour
- 1 teaspoon salt
- 1 teaspoon baking soda
- 2 cups quick-cooking oats
- 1 cup walnuts or pecans (optional)
- 1 cup chocolate chips (and/or raisins)

DIRECTIONS:

Cream shortenings and sugars and add eggs and vanilla. Beat well. Sift together flour, salt, and soda. Add these dry ingredients to the creamed mixture. Blend in slowly and mix well. Add remaining ingredients and blend thoroughly. Separate into two parts, roll in waxed paper, and chill for several hours. Slice and place on ungreased cookie sheet. Bake at 325 degrees for approximately ten minutes or until light brown. Cool on paper towels. Makes about four dozen.

"I first developed this recipe when I was working as a Mathematical engineer in California. One of my co-workers told me that he liked my oatmeal cookies better than his mother's, but he liked her chocolate chip cookies better than mine. He suggested that I try to incorporate chocolate chips and whatever else I thought would work in my oatmeal cookies. This is the result, and the recipe was even shared along with my picture in the Atlanta Journal and Constitution paper.

"I am the Dillard President's mother and am retired from being a mathematical engineer, software manager and consultant, college professor, and published author."

MRS. GLINSEY'S LEMON SUPREME CAKE

Bertha Glinsey
Chicago, IL
Homemaker, 84 years old

INGREDIENTS:

- 1 box of Duncan Hines Lemon Supreme Cake mix
- 1 (8 ounce) regular frozen lemonade
- ½ cup of powdered white sugar

DIRECTIONS:

Follow the recipe instructions on the box. Mix 4 ounces of frozen lemonade and ½ cup of powdered white sugar. The lemonade sugar mixture will turn into a paste. Remove cake 5 minutes before the directed time. With a plastic cake spatula spread the lemonade sugar mixture over the entire cake. Let the cake cool for 30 minutes and serve. Mrs. Glinsey has been making this recipe for sixty years for friends and family.

SOUTHERN PECAN CHEESECAKE

Zella Palmer
New Orleans, LA
Chair, Dillard University Ray Charles Program

INGREDIENTS:

- 4 bars of room temperature
    Philly cream cheese
- 3 eggs
- 2 cups of packed brown sugar
- 1 teaspoon of vanilla
- 2 sticks of butter
- 1 cup of graham cracker crumbs
- 2 cups of pecans
- ⅓ cup of good maple syrup

DIRECTIONS:

Melt 1 stick of butter. Mix 1 cup of Graham cracker crumbs, butter, and 1 teaspoon of brown sugar. Add the graham cracker mixture to the bottom of a springform pan and press down with a flat spoon until it is a flat layer of crust. In a mixing bowl, add two bars of Philly cream cheese and 1 egg. Mix with electric mixer. Add 1 cup of brown sugar. Mix. Add two more bars of Philly cream cheese and two remaining eggs. Mix. Add vanilla. Taste. Add cream cheese mixture to the springform pan. Bake cheesecake for 1 hour in a preheated 350 degree oven. Cool, then refrigerate for 4 hours. In a saucepan, melt butter on low heat. Add a pinch of vanilla and pecans. Remove from heat. In a mixing bowl. Mix the pecans with ⅓ cup of good maple syrup. Spread the pecan mixture over the refrigerated cream cheesecake. Put a plate under the springform pan to catch the syrup drippings. Refrigerate overnight. Remove the springform and serve.

· ·

KEY LIME CAKE

Mrs. Adria N. Kimbrough, Esq.
New Orleans, LA, Dillard University
First Lady and Pre-Law Advisor,
Center for Law and Public Interest

INGREDIENTS:

- (18.25-ounce) package lemon cake mix
- 1 ⅓ cups vegetable oil
- 4 eggs
- 1 (3-ounce) package lime flavored Jell-O mix
- ¾ cup orange juice
- ½ cup butter
- 1 (8-ounce) package cream cheese
- 3 tablespoons fresh lime juice
- 4 cups confectioners' sugar

DIRECTIONS:

Combine cake mix, gelatin mix, oil, eggs, and orange juice. Pour into three 8-inch cake pans. Bake according to instructions on box. Allow to cool, then frost.

For Frosting: In a large bowl, beat the butter and cream cheese until light and fluffy. Add lime juice and confectioners sugar. Mix well.

MADAME BARBARA TREVIGNE
BELLE CALAS

Madame Barbara Trevigne
New Orleans, LA
New Orleans Historian

INGREDIENTS:

- 2 cups of mushy cold rice
- 6 teaspoons of flour
- 3 heaping tablespoons of sugar
- 2 teaspoons of baking powder
- ¼ teaspoon of salt
- ¼ teaspoon of vanilla
- ½ teaspoon of fresh nutmeg
- Powdered sugar
- 3 eggs
- Peanut oil or vegetable oil

DIRECTIONS:

Mix the cold mushy rice and dry ingredients together thoroughly. Add the eggs and when thoroughly mixed, drop by spoonful into hot deep oil in 360 degree temperature. Fry until golden brown and drain on brown paper bag. Sprinkle liberally with powdered sugar. Serve hot. Calas should never be eaten cold.

Overcook the rice the day before and keep in refrigerator. Maintain mixture below 70 degrees because the batter will separate when dropped in the hot oil. If you are planning on cooking lots of Calas, be sure to keep the ingredients in the refrigerator. If not, the consistency of the mixture will become watery and separate. It has to remain cold.

CALAS SONG:

Tout chaud calas, Tout chaud calas
Belle calas, Belle calas
Tout Chaud Calas, donnez moi un picayune,
Belle Calas, Monsieur et Madame. Pour vous.

Merchants in New Orleans frequently called and sang out their items for sale to attract customers. One popular vendor was the calas lady. The calas lady could be found selling her delicious calas near the St. Louis Cathedral Catholic Church, or walking along the levee by the Mississippi River. Each merchant sang a catchy tune about their item to attract the housewife. When the call of the vendor was heard, women do-popped (peeping through their shutters) and came out to inspect and purchase the goods. Not only were there food merchants, there was the rag man, the fruit man, and the cowan man who traveled first by mule-drawn carts, which graduated to trucks. It was the cadence of their songs and the freshness of their food that made a good dinner. Calas was breakfast Mardi Gras morning and after First Communion (Little Communion), with hot chocolate.

The memory of my maternal grandmother Emily Broyard Trevigne making calas, and the smell of her calas, fill my heart with joy. The simplicity of food makes a family gathering a treasure trove of love.

HONEY BREAD PUDDING WITH CHOCOLATE DRIZZLE

V. Sheree Williams
Los Angeles, CA
Publisher, *Cuisine Noir* Magazine

INGREDIENTS:

- 1 cup of Honey Ridge Farms Coconut Honey or honey, melted and divided
- 2 eggs
- 1 tablespoon of vanilla
- 1 tablespoon of cinnamon
- ¼ teaspoon of salt
- ¼ cup of sugar
- ½ cup of walnuts
- ½ cup of raisins
- 6 cups of bread, small cubes
- ¼ cup of butter
- 2 cups of milk
- ¼ cup of milk chocolate morsels, melted

DIRECTIONS:

Heat oven to 375 degrees. In a small saucepan, add ½ cup honey and melt down just slightly. Pour into a ramekin and set aside. In a large mixing bowl, add the eggs, vanilla, cinnamon, salt, sugar, melted honey, walnuts, and raisins. Mix until blended.

Add in bread slowly until as much as possible is covered with the mixture. In a medium saucepan, heat the milk and butter until the butter is melted. Pour over bread and mix everything together. To get a hint of the flavor, taste with a tasting spoon and add a little extra vanilla or cinnamon if needed. Pour mixture into a 9 x 9 square baking dish. Place in oven and bake for 45 minutes or until a toothpick insert comes out clean. In a saucepan, melt chocolate morsels and pour into piping bag or ramekin. Set aside. With a honey wand, drizzle the rest of the honey around the bread pudding. Next, pipe the melted chocolate around as well. You can also just use a spoon. Cut and enjoy hot with some vanilla bean ice cream

• •

OLD FASHIONED PINEAPPLE SHERBERT

Gisele Perez
New Orleans, LA
Pain Perdu Blog

INGREDIENTS:

- 3 ½ cups of canned, crushed pineapple packed in juice, along with the juice
- 5 ounces of sweetened condensed milk
- 1 teaspoon of freshly squeezed lemon juice
- 2 egg whites
- 1 pinch of salt

DIRECTIONS:

Combine pineapple, sweetened condensed milk, and lemon juice in a bowl and chill in the refrigerator for several hours, or overnight. In a separate bowl, beat the egg whites with a pinch of salt. Take the chilled mixture from the refrigerator and fold in the beaten egg whites in 3 additions. Freeze in an ice cream maker according to your machine's directions. The sherbet will be soft. It may be served as is, or placed in a freezer to freeze harder.

FRESH STRAWBERRY SHORTBREAD

Mary Louise Thomas
Bayou Lafourche, LA
Former Chef and Owner
New Orleans Mais Oui: Creole & Soul Food Restaurant

INGREDIENTS:

- 2 pints of fresh ripe Louisiana strawberries
- 2 cups of self-rising flour
- ½ cup of sugar
- 8 tablespoons of Crisco
- ½ cup of sugar
- 3 eggs
- 3 tablespoons of water
- 2 teaspoons of water
- 2 teaspoons of vanilla
- ½ cup of sugar
- ¼ cup of water

DIRECTIONS:

Preheat oven to 400 degrees. Wash strawberries. Pinch stems to remove. Cut each berry in half. Place berries into a bowl. Sprinkle water and sugar over berries. Mix with fingers to avoid bruising the berries. Cover and refrigerate until ready to use. Berries should be refrigerated for at least 24 hours with sugar to make juice.

Combine Crisco, sugar, eggs, and vanilla. Add flour then water, blending all ingredients together. Roll dough onto a lightly floured surface ¼-inch thick. Cut into 5-inch circles. Place shortcakes on a dusted baking sheet. Bake in a pre-heated 400 degree oven for 10 minutes.

Top the short bread with the strawberries. Spoon some of the strawberry juice over berries and shortbread. Top with whipped cream or Cool Whip.

. . . .

BANANA MACADAMIA NUT BREAD

Dr. Yolanda W. Page
New Orleans, LA, Dillard University
Vice-President, Academic Affairs

INGREDIENTS:

- 2 cups flour
- ¾ cup sugar
- 2 eggs
- 1 teaspoon vanilla
- 1 cup mashed banana
- 1 cup coconut flakes
- ½ cup of sweet creamy butter
- 1 tablespoon baking soda
- ½ teaspoon salt
- 1 tablespoon grated orange peel
- ¼ cup orange juice
- ¾ cup walnuts

DIRECTIONS:

Heat oven to 350 degrees. Combine flour, eggs, sugar, butter, salt, baking soda, and vanilla. Beat at low speed, 2–3 minutes or with a whisk. Add bananas and orange juice. Continue beating for another minute. Stir in coconut and nuts. Spread into greased loaf pan. Bake for 60–65 minutes. Allow to cool before slicing.

HUCKLEBUCKS

Dr. Mona Lisa Saloy
New Orleans, LA, Dillard University
Author and Endowed Professor, English

Hucklebucks are a sweet treat popular for many years from New Orleans to Georgia. Exported North during the Great Migrations, in Detroit they are called "Dixie Cups," so called for the Dixie-cup brand used from its mid-twentieth century kids-sized cup used for the frozen confection. Others just say "frozen cup."

Historically, in hot climates, frozen hard drinks became more common for everyone after the turn of the twentieth century with the advent of ice wagons carting ice to neighborhoods. As soon as those large blocks of ice were purchased by many businesses, the paper-cone cups held a fill of the crushed or "shaved" ice, crowned by a dome and layered atop with syrup of one or various fruit flavors. Even though "snow cones" or "snowballs" were an inexpensive, cold, and sweet treat, in the days of dollar-a-week work (growing to dollar-a-day labor prior to the Great Depression), in semi-tropical New Orleans, a homemade cold and sweet treat became the salvation of working-class families short of two nickels to rub together. Still, we had to have snow cones or snowballs. This necessity birthed the creative confection now known as Hucklebucks, which came into general use with the affordability and ability to house ice at home in iceboxes, then later, refrigerators. We all made them at home. When one family made a big batch, folks shared with all the kids on the block in turn. We shared our Hucklebucks.

Originally made with frozen lemonade, fruit juice, or flavor added to pure cane syrup, some families added chunks of pineapple to the mix for an added fruity touch. Then, by mid-twentieth century and the affordability of nickel packs of Kool-Aid, folks just added sugar to the colored, flavored water to make many Hucklebucks or Frozen Cups, since one pack of Kool-Aid makes a gallon. Even to those, people added pineapple or, on occasion, diced fruit from cans, popularly called fruit cocktail. For a simple Hucklebuck, nothing else is needed. Also, once we had a refrigerator, and if we ran out of small paper cups, we made the frozen treat into cubes from the ice cube trays, great hand-size for little ones.

DIRECTIONS: Take six large or medium tart lemons. Squeeze all the juice out of them into a half-gallon pitcher; yes, use the pulp, which will keep it tasty and tart. Add half to a whole cup of sugar or sweeten to taste; how much will depend on the tartness of the lemons. Stir strongly to dissolve all sugar. Honey or Maple syrup can replace sugar. Then pour the lemonade into small paper or plastic cups. Place the filled cups into the freezer until frozen solid. How long depends on the coldness of the fridge.

While Kool-Aid makes a great variety of colors for Hucklebucks, easily pour your favorite ready-made fruit juice into small cups (size depends on your preference) to freeze. My favorite is to freeze cranberry juice or coconut-pineapple juice, oooooo good.

Today, there's a Hucklebuck lady in the historic 7th Ward of New Orleans, where Dillard University resides. Folks pay for her treats, but most of us still make Hucklebucks at home.

BLEU DEVIL COLADA

Michelle M. Mathews
New Orleans, LA, Dillard University
Manager of Auxiliary Services

INGREDIENTS:

- 1 package of Kool-Aid mix,
  Blue Raspberry Lemonade flavor
- 1 ½ cups of granulated sugar
- 1 liter of Sprite
- 1 quart of cold water
- 16 ounces of non-alcoholic
  Pina Colada drink mix
- Maraschino cherries
  and grated coconut for garnish
- Royal blue sugar for glass rimming

DIRECTIONS:

Mix Kool-Aid packet, sugar, Sprite, and cold water until sugar is dissolved well. In a blender, fill with ice and add 16 ounces of drink mixture. Blend until smooth. Rim glass with sugar and fill with mixture. Add cherries on an umbrella and finely grated coconut to garnish.

 Bleu Devil Colada is the official Dillard University drink that is served at special events.

AMARETTO PUNCH

M. Shannon Williamson, M.S.
New Orleans, LA, Dillard University
Assistant Director, Academic Center for Excellence

INGREDIENTS:

- 1 cup of sugar
- 4 ½ cups of water
- 1 can lemonade, frozen, thawed (6 ounces)
- 1 can orange juice, frozen, thawed (6 ounces)
- 1 can pineapple juice, frozen, thawed (6 ounces)
- 1 cup of amaretto
- 2 liters ginger ale
- Maraschino cherries (optional)

DIRECTIONS:

Combine sugar and water in saucepan. Stir well, bring to a boil. Reduce heat, simmer 15 minutes, stirring occasionally. Remove from heat and allow mixture to cool. Combine sugar mixture, lemonade, orange juice, pineapple juice, and amaretto/almond syrup. Stir well. Freeze mixture overnight. Break into chunks. Add ginger ale and cherries. Yields 16 cups.

 For non-alcoholic version substitute 1 cup of almond syrup used at coffee shops.

BRAZILIAN LEMONADE

Zella Palmer
New Orleans, LA
Chair, Dillard University Ray Charles Program

INGREDIENTS:

- 6 squeezed lemons
- ½ cup of sweetened condensed milk
- 3 cups of water
- Ice
- Sugar
- Fresh mint

DIRECTIONS:

Squeeze lemons. Remove seeds and pulp and add to a medium size pitcher. Add 3 cups of water. Stir. Add sweetened condensed milk. Stir. Add ⅓ cup of sugar. Taste and adjust sugar level. Serve lemonade with ice and garnish with fresh mint.

STRAWBERRY BASIL LEMONADE

Zella Palmer
New Orleans, LA
Chair, Dillard University Ray Charles Program

INGREDIENTS:

- 6 squeezed lemons, 2 cups of lemon juice
- 2 cups of sugar
- 3 cups of water
- 1 cup of ripe strawberries
- 2 sprigs of fresh basil
- Ice

DIRECTIONS:

In a large pitcher, with a pestle or wooden spoon, crush strawberries and fresh basil. Add lemon juice, water, and sugar. Adjust sugar level. Refrigerate overnight and serve with ice.

GRANDMOTHER CATHERINE'S KENTUCKY EGGNOG

Dr. Alice J. Palmer
Chicago, IL

INGREDIENTS:

- 8 eggs, separated
- 2 cups of sugar
- 1–1 ½ cups bourbon (optional)
- 1 teaspoon vanilla extract
- 5 ½ pints whipping cream

DIRECTIONS:

Separate egg yolks and whites. Beat egg yolks and add sugar. Add bourbon and vanilla. Blend well. Beat whipped cream and add to egg yolks and bourbon. Beat egg whites until stiff. Fold into egg yolks, bourbon, whipped cream mixture. Dust with nutmeg.

Introduction Endnotes

1. James D. Browne, ed. "What's in a Name," *Dillard University Courtbouillon*, December 6, 1935.

2. Charles H. Loeb, for the *Washington Afro-American*, June 1, 1954.

3. Theodore M. Vestal, *The Lion of Judah in the New World: Emperor Haile Selassie of Ethiopia and the Shaping of Americans' Attitudes toward Africa* (New York: Praeger, 2011), 83.

4. Loeb, *Washington Afro-American*, June 1, 1954.

5. Vestal, *Lion of Judah.*

6. Ibid.

7. Loeb, *Washington Afro-American*, June 1, 1954.

8. *Dillard University Women's Club Cookbook* (New Orleans: Dillard University, 1958).

9. "Albert W. Dent Dead; Led Dillard University," *The New York Times*, February 13, 1984, accessed February 3, 2015, http://www.nytimes.com/1984/02/14/obituaries/albert-w-dent-dead-led-dillard-university.html.

10. Kalamu ya Salaam, Phone interview with Zella Palmer, New Orleans, January 15, 2015.

11. Ibid.

12. Michael Patrick Welch, "Before Jazz Fest, There Was the Afro-American Arts Festival," New Orleans *Louisiana Weekly*, April 20, 2015: n. pag. Web. July 22, 2016.

13. *The Dillard University Auxiliary International Food Festival Cookbook* (New Orleans: Dillard University, 197?).

14. Marc Barnes, Interview with Zella Palmer, New Orleans, February 3, 2015.

15. Dillard Today

16. Jarrett Carter, "Dillard Brings Brain Food To The Masses With Renowned HBCU Lecture Series," *Huffington Post*, accessed February 3, 2015, http://www.huffingtonpost.com/2014/01/31/dillard-university_n_4705630.html.

17. Nathaniel Burton and Rudy Lombard, *Creole Feast: 15 Master Chefs of New Orleans Reveal Their Secrets* (New York: Random House, 1978), 19.

Image Credits

x-xi: Table spread of recipes cooked by Chef Edgar Dooky Chase Jr. III, photo by Jeremy Shine; xii: Dillard University campus, photo by Jeremy Shine; xiii: Walter Kimbrough, courtesy of My New Orleans; xiv: Leah Chase's gumbo, photo by Jeremy Shine; xv: Flint-Goodridge Hospital, courtesy of Amistad Research Center; xvii: Author Zella Palmer and Leah Chase, courtesy of Zella Palmer; xviii: Grillades, photo by Jeremy Shine; 1: Portrait of Straight University class of 1896, courtesy of Amistad Research Center; 2: Dillard President Dent and Mrs. Eleanor Roosevelt at WDSU studio, 1953, courtesy of Amistad Research Center; Bottom: Mr. Stern, Emperor Haile Selassie I, Albert W. Dent, Mayor DeLesseps Story Morrison, photo Credit Longvue House and Gardens, courtesy of Amistad Research Center; 3: The banquet honoring Haile Selassie at the International House, June 24, 1954. Third from left, Haile Selassie, and fourth from left, Mrs. deLesseps Morrison, courtesy of Amistad Research Center; Bottom: Photograph from banquet honoring Haile Selassie, courtesy of Amistad Research Center; 4: Cover for the The Dillard Women's Club Cookbook, courtesy of Amistad Research Center; Bottom: Alpha Kappa Alpha – Alpha Beta Omega chapter with Marian Anderson, 1941, courtesy of Amistad Research Center; 5: Advertisements from local New Orleans businesses in the Dillard Women's Club Cookbook, courtesy of Amistad Research Center; 6: Aerial view of Dillard, December 1961, courtesy of Amistad Research Center; 7: Dr. Samuel DuBois Cook, from the interior of The Dillard University Auxiliary International Food Festival Cookbook, courtesy of Dillard University Ray Charles Program; Below: The Dillard University Auxiliary International Food Festival Cookbook cover, courtesy of Dillard University Ray Charles Program; 9: Brain food menu from 2016, courtesy of the Dillard University Ray Charles Program in African-American Material Culture; Below: Dillard University campus, 2019, courtesy of Zella Palmer; 10: Cooking demo, courtesy of the Dillard University Ray Charles Program in African-American Material Culture; Below: Students in restaurant, courtesy of Glenn Rebert; 11: Mardi Gras Indian Queen Cherice Harrison Nelson and mother Hearest Harrison passing down recipes to the next generation, courtesy of the Dillard University Ray Charles Program in African-American Material Culture; Below: Mrs. Adria Nobles Kimbrough at cooking demo with key lime pie, courtesy of the Dillard University Ray Charles Program in African-American Material Culture; 12: Redfish courtbouiliion, photo by Jeremy Shine; 13: Below: Page from Dent family guestbook with Duke Ellington, Jackie Robinson, and Jim Brown as guest entries, courtesy of Amistad Research Center; 14: Page from Dent family guestbook with Haile Selassie's signature, courtesy of Amistad Research Center; Below: Reverend Elliot Mason speaking at an alumni dinner hosted by the Dents, courtesy of Amistad Research Center; 15: Dent family photo, courtesy of Amistad Research Center; 16: Letter from the Women's Club detailing plans for a cookbook, courtesy of Amistad Research Center; 17: Front cover for Dillard Women's Club Cookbook, courtesy of Amistad Research Center; 18: "Recipe for a Good Life" from Women's Cookbook, courtesy of Amistad Research Center; 20: "Eleanor Roosevelt at United Nations in Paris, November 1951," courtesy of Franklin D. Roosevelt Library (NLFDR), https://commons.wikimedia.org/wiki/File:Eleanor_Roosevelt_at_United_Nations_in_Paris_-_NARA_-_195965_(cropped).jpg; 21: Photograph of Marian Anderson, 1936, from Negro musicians and their music by Maud Cuney-Hare. Washington, D.C.: The Associated Publishers, Inc., 1936, p. 357, courtesy of https://commons.wikimedia.org/wiki/File:Maud_Cuney_Hare-Marian_Anderson_357.jpg; 22: "Mary McLeod Bethune, 6 April, 1949," courtesy of Library of Congress's Prints and Photographs division, https://commons.wikimedia.org/wiki/File:Mary_McLeod_Bethune_(1949).jpg 23: Ralph J. Bunche, photographed by Carl Van Vechten, 1951, courtesy of Library of Congress's Prints and Photographs division, https://commons.wikimedia.org/wiki/File:Ralph_Bunche,_1951.jpg; 23, below: "Publicity photo of soprano Mattiwilda Dobbs. 13 October 1957," courtesy of https://commons.wikimedia.org/wiki/File:Mattiwilda_Dobbs_1957.JPG; 24: Natalie Hinderas, courtesy of Zella Palmer; 25: "Photo of Lena Horne. 31 March 1955, Metro Goldwyn Mayer," courtesy of https://commons.wikimedia.org/wiki/File:Lena_Horne_1955.JPG; 26: Charles S. Johnson, courtesy of Amistad Research Center; 29: Theodore

K. Lawless, courtesy of the Amistad Research Center; 30: "Photograph of Etta Moten, 1936," from *Negro musicians and their music* by Maud Cuney-Hare. Washington, D.C.: The Associated Publishers, Inc., 1936, p. 378, courtesy of https://commons.wikimedia.org/wiki/File:Maud_Cuney_Hare-378-Etta_Moten.jpg; 31: "Charlotte Wallace Murray– 1940," courtesy of Vieilles Annonces, https://www.flickr.com/photos/vieilles_annonces/4987559683; Below: "Camille Nickerson," In *https://64parishes.org Encyclopedia of Louisiana*, edited by David Johnson, Louisiana Endowment for the Humanities, 2010, Article published August 8, 2013, https://64parishes.org/entry/camille-nickerson, Smithsonian Archives of American Art; 33: "Philippa Schuyler, concert pianist. 1959," courtesy of the Library of Congress, New York World-Telegram & Sun Collection, http://hdl.loc.gov/loc.pnp/cph.3c09640; 34: Howard Thurman, courtesy of the Amistad Research Center.; 35: Leontyne Price and William Warfield, courtesy of the Amistad Research Center; 36: "J. Ernest Wilkins - Assistant Secretary of Labor, 1954-58," courtesy of https://commons.wikimedia.org/wiki/File:J._Ernest_Wilkins_Sr._-Assistant_Secretary_of_Labor_-U.S._Government_portrait_V3_-cropped-.jpg; 126: Crawfish bisque at table setting, photo by Jeremy Shine; 128: Portrait of students outside of school building, 1977, courtesy of the Amistad Research Center; 129: Front cover for Dillard Auxiliary's International Food Festival Cookbook, courtesy of Dillard University Ray Charles Program; 158: Linda Green's Jambalaya, photo by Jeremy Shine; 160: Food demo with Mrs. Adria Nobles Kimbrough, photos by Sabree Hill; 162: Daube Glace, photo by Jeremy Shine; 165: Seafood Gumbo, photo by Jeremy Shine; 166: Grits and Grillades, photo by Jeremy Shine; 171: Linda Green's Red Beans and Rice, photo by Jeremy Shine; 173: Crawfish Bisque, photo by Jeremy Shine; 174: Linda Green's Jambalaya, photo by Jeremy Shine; 178: Stuffed Crab, photo by Jeremy Shine; 200: Italian Cream Cake, photo by Sabree Hill; 207: Blue Devil Colada, photo by Jeremy Shine

RECIPE INDEX

THE DILLARD WOMEN'S CLUB COOKBOOK

A FEW FAVORITE RECIPES FROM A FEW FAMOUS FRIENDS

Huckleberry Dessert Eleanor Roosevelt...................................20
South American Pudding Marian Anderson...........................21
Old Fashioned Brown Sugar Cookies Dr. Mary Mcleod Bethune........22
Creamed Sweetbreads Ralph J. Bunche..............................23
Jansson's Temptation Mattiwilda Dobbs............................23
Le Nouveau Riche Poule Natalie Hinderas..........................24
East Indian Chicken Lena Horne...................................25
Virginia Gentleman Steak Dinner Mrs. Charles S. Johnson..........26
Italian Spaghetti Toki Schalk Johnson............................27
Spiced Chicken Legs Freda De Knight..............................28
Ginger Bread – Hot Cakes of Honolulu Theodore K. Lawless.........29
Ravioli Casserole Mr. And Mrs. William H. Mitchell Jr. 29
Indonesian Chicken (African Groundnut Stew) Etta Moten...........30
Standard Blueberry Muffins Mrs. Charlotte Wallace Murray.........31
Pain Patate Camille Lucie Nickerson..............................31
Crab Meat a la Capahosic Fred D. Patterson.......................32
Bacon Eggs and Mushrooms Ira De Augustine Reid...................32
Autumn Joy Philippa Duke Schuyler................................33
Eggs Benedict William J. Trent Jr................................33
"12th Night Wassail" Howard And Sue Bailey Thurman...............34
Spinach Balls Mrs. Robert L. Vann................................35
Champignons au Vin Leontyne Price And William Warfield...........35
Potato Splits Mrs. J. Ernest Wilkins.............................36
Plain Muffins Miss Fannie C. Williams............................36

AROUND THE WORLD RECIPES

Canton Pork with Pineapple Sauce Dr. Sauk Wong...................38
Almond Coffee Torte Mrs. Wilma Iggers............................38
Christmas Pudding Mrs. Linda Furey...............................39
Yorkshire Pudding Mrs. Linda Furey...............................39
Wine Pot Roast Geddes Jones......................................40
A Harvey Home Special – Musaka Clarie Harvey.....................40
Chiffon Pie Mrs. Wilbur S. Wood..................................41
Biriani Dr. Gourie Mukherjee.....................................41
Chicken Fried Rice Yvonne Mason Burbridge........................42
Chatazilim – Eggplant Aubergine The Israeli Embassy..............42
Bird Nest Pie Henrine Ward Banks.................................43
Baroness Pudding Florence Fraser.................................43
Chawan Mush (Steamed Chicken Custard) Mrs. Galen Russell.........44

Sukiyaki Mrs. Charles S. Johnson 44

Jollof Rice Mrs. Prince A. Taylor 45

Liberian Perlieu Rice Mrs. Louise Yancy 45

Chicken Curry with Rice Mildred Hastings Swerdlow 46

Enchiladas Mrs. Margaret Simms 46

Beef Stroganoff Mrs. Samuel C. Kincheloe 47

Chicken Breasts "Villaroy' Mattiwilda Dobbs 47

Turkish Delight Phillipa Duke Schuyler 48

Easy Hamburgers or Meat Loaf Louise Prothro 48

CREOLE RECIPES

Calas (Rice Cakes) Mildred Hastings Swerdlow 50

Courtbouillon a la Creole Mrs. Edward E. Moore 50

Crab Cutlets Mrs. Julia Duncan 51

Crab a la Casserole Mrs. Lydia G. Sindos 52

Deviled Crabs Mrs. Bona V. Arnaud 52

Crayfish Bisque Mrs. Anita Gilbert 53

Crayfish Bisque Mrs. C. C. Haydel 53

Fish a la Harriet Mrs. Harriett Holmes 54

Fish Filet Casserole Mrs. Lena Forcia Landry 54

Warren's Southern Jambalaya Mrs. Christine Warren 55

Oysters a la Poulette Mrs. Julia Duncan 55

Cawain (Soft Shell Turtle Stew) Mrs. Ella Rieras 56

Oignons Glaces (Glazed Onions) Mildred Hastings Swerdlow 56

Shrimp Creole Mrs. Juliet Walker-Mitchell 57

Shrimp Balls Mrs. Ernest Cherrie 57

Shrimp Remoulade Mrs. Daisy Hatter 58

Grillades Mrs. Lydia G. Sindos 58

Gumbo Z'herbes Mrs. Ernest Cherrie 59

Creole Gumbo with Okra Mrs. August Terrence 59

Eggplant with Crabmeat Mrs. Bona V. Arnaud 60

Homemade Tomato Catsup Phyllis Champion 60

Pecan Pralines Mrs. Bona V. Arnaud 61

Creamy Creole Chocolate Fudge Mrs. Natalie Forcia 61

LOUISIANA YAMS AROUND THE CLOCK: PIES, CAKES, VEGETABLES, ETC.

Yam Tomato Bisque 64

Yam Nut Muffins 64

Louisiana Griddle Cakes 65

Orange Sweet Potatoes Mrs. Margaret Colteryahn 65

Minted Yam and Pineapple Bake 66

Baked Stuffed Yams with Brandy 66

Sweet Potato Pie Mrs. Charles S. Johnson 67

Yam Cocoanut Pie...67
Sweet Potato Pudding..68
Yam Apricot Sherbet..68

APPETIZERS, PICKLES, AND RELISH

Avocado Dip Mrs. Tibbye Thomas...70
Cheese Puffs Grace Lepine...70
Chopped Liver (Gehakte Leber) Mrs. Charles Swerdlow..................70
Egg Cushions Mrs. I. M. Mitchell..71
Watermelon Pickles Mrs. Floyd Morgan.................................71
Red Pepper Jam Miss Helen Albro.......................................71
Scampi Mrs. Lucile Segre...72
Welsh Rarebit Grace Lepin..72

SOUP, SALADS, SAUCES, DRESSINGS

Cold Vegetable Soup Mrs. Claire Harvey................................74
Fish Chowder Mrs. William N. Davis.....................................74
Vichysoisse Ebony Test Kitchen..74
Avocado with Lobster Mrs. Lucile Segre.................................75
Avocado and Shrimp Salad Mildred Hastings Swerdlow.................75
Chicken Royal Salad Mrs. Irene Waters.................................76
Entrée Mrs. Carrie Johnson..76
Pineapple Cottage Cheese Salad Mrs. Jesse O. Richards................76
Seafood Mold Mrs. Edith Brooks..77
Fruit and Vegetable Salad Essie Williams...............................77
Butterscotch Sauce Mrs. J. Colomb.......................................77
French Chili Sauce Mrs. Alice Jones Tull................................78
Green Sauce for Fish and Seafood Geddes Jones......................78
French Dressing Mrs. Vivian Green.......................................78
Oyster Sauce Jessie C. Dent..79
Cornish Hen Sauce Ebony Test Kitchen..................................79

MAIN DISHES—MEAT, SEAFOOD, POULTRY

Anybody's Stew Alvin S. Bynum...82
Stuffed Ham Mrs. Harriet Holmes..82
Baked Pig Mrs. Anita Gilbert..83
Pork Chops with Oyster Stuffing Mrs. P. Q. Yancy....................83
Sour Rabbit (or Hasenpfeffer) Mrs. Margaret Colteryahn.............84
Deviled Lobster Mrs. Christine Warren..................................84
Creamed Oysters Mrs. M. S. Davage......................................85
Chatter Ebon' Ebony Test Kitchen..85
Shrimp and Artichoke Newburg Mrs. Anita Gilbert...................86
Guinea Hens Mrs. Juliet Walker Mitchell................................86

Stuffed Capon Mrs. Marie E. Burbridge 87
Hungarian Chicken Paprika Mrs. Lenora Cooper 87
Spanish Rest Mrs. Mable Armstrong 88
Duckling in Aspic Mrs. Mary E. Slade.. 88
Roast Wild Duck (Teal Or French) Mrs. E. Lyons Baker...................... 89
Rock Cornish Hen with Rice Dressing Coragreene Johnstone.......... 89
Curried Chicken Mildred Hastings Swerdlow 90
Fruit of the Bayou Mrs. Daisy Young 90
Cold Fish Platter Harriette Holmes.. 90

Main Dishes—Cheese, Egg, Spaghetti, Casserole

Stuffed Eggs Mrs. Emile Blanchard 92
Chicken and Spaghetti Supreme Mrs. Henrietta Johnson 92
Hominy au Gratin Mrs. Margaret Simms 93
Spaghetti with Mushrooms Mrs. Malcolm Mcdonald 93
Tuna Tetrazzini Mrs. Frances Gandy... 94
Oyster and Corn Casserole Mrs. Irene Edmonds.................................... 94
Red Bean Casserole Mrs. Tibbye Thomas 95
Deluxe Cauliflower Casserole Mrs. Lenora Cooper 95
Turkey Casserole Mrs. Mary E. Slade.. 96
Company Casserole Miss Ethel Mae Griggs.. 96

Vegetables

Celery Hearts with Special Tomato Sauce Mrs. Mabel Armstrong 98
Corn Pudding Mrs. Anne Teabeau 98
Stuffed Eggplant Mrs. P. Q. Yancey 99
West Indian Scalloped Potatoes Mrs. Lenora Cooper 99
Rice – "Elegant Variations" Coragreene Johnstone 100
Spinach Surprise Ebony Test Kitchen 101
Succotash Mrs. Carmen Robinson.. 101
Stewed Tomatoes Mrs. Charles S. Johnson 102
Sweet and Sour Green Beans Mildred Hastings Swerdlow.................. 102
Stuffed Mirlitons (Vegetable Pear) Mae Colomb............................... 103

Bread, Rolls, Pies, and Pastry

Banana Bread Mrs. Robert E. Jones... 106
Corn Bread with a Future Ebony Test Kitchen 106
Cream Puffs Anita Gilbert 107
Old Fashioned Nut Loaf Mrs. Emilie Blanchard................................... 107
Honey Bran Rolls Ms. Murnetta Johnson... 108
Hot Rolls Mrs. Vera Codwell 108
Ice Box Rolls Mrs. Malvina Williams 109
Spoon Bread Mildred Hastings Swerdlow 109

Fruit Cobbler Mrs. B. J. Covington 110
Lemon Meringue Pie Whaley Jessie.. 110
Lemon and Raisin Pie Miss Helen Yeomans...............................111
Meringue Apple Pie Mrs. A. M. Bynum 111
Pecan Pie Helen Mcclain 112
Gelatin Rum Cream Pie Mrs. Verna Chambers................................ 112

Cakes, Cookies And Icings

Banana Spice Cake Mrs. Edith Brooks 114
Blackberry Jam Cake Mrs. Mildred Crawford 115
Black Chocolate Cake Mrs. Hertha Taylor................................ 115
Cheesecake Mrs. Daisy Blanchet 116
Chocolate Ice Box Cake Mrs. Kenneth Herreld 116
Chocolate Malted Milk Cake Mrs. Alice Jones Tull 117
Ruth's Pound Cake Mrs. Ruth Betsill Johnstone 117
Pineapple Upside Down Cake Mrs. Willis J. King................... 118
Butter Cookies Mrs. Adam Ratliff.. 118
Butter Cookies Supreme Miss Vera Jenkins 119
Butterscotch Slices Mrs. Alice Tull 119
Cinnamon Refrigerator Cookies Mrs. Gertrude Holmes 120
Date and Nut Chews Mrs. Edith Brooks 120
Macaroons Mrs. Amelia Linton 121
Aunt Amy's Cookies Miss Virginia Cates................................ 121

Desserts

Delicious Ice Cream Margaret Davis Bowen 122
Coffee Ice Cream Mrs. Emma Brown...................................... 122
Pearl's Special Dessert Mrs. Pearl Gore 122
Date Souffle Mrs. Harriet Holmes 123
Mrs. Trundy's Indian Pudding Mrs. Walter P. Colteryahn 123
Lemon Delight Mrs. Julia Duncan 124
Cake Top Lemon Pudding Mrs. Juliet Walker-Mitchell 124
Mocha Souffle Mrs. Harriet Holmes 125
Delicous Old-Fashioned Bread Pudding Estelle Turpin.................... 125

Dillard Auxiliary's
International Food Festival Cookbook

African

Corned Beef Stew Mr. Christian Fugar....................................... 131
Fried Plantain Mr. Christian Fugar.. 131

Fried Yams Mr. Christian Fugar 131
Ground Nut Stew Dr. Shelby Faye Lewis.. 132
Moi Moi Azubike Okpalaeze 132
Jollof Rice Dr. Anthony Osei... 133
Spinach Stew Dr. Anthony Osei... 133

AMERICAN

Clam Dip Dr. Winona Somervill 134
Green Bean Casserole (Texas Style) Dr. Bennie Webster 134

ASIAN-AMERICAN

Fried Egg Roll Mrs. Marivic D. Ortiz-Luis 135
Chinese Chicken (Teno Style) Mrs. Elois Teno 135

CREOLE/CAJUN

Grillades Mrs. Marie Wiggan Houston 136
Crawfish Bisque Ms. Karen Lawrence Pleas 136
Jambalaya Mrs. Dorothy S. Randolph 137
Catfish Fingers in Garlic Sauce Patricia Saul Rochon...................... 138
New Orleans French Market Bean Soup Dr. Jeffery Smith 138
Jude's Boiled Crawfish Dr. Jude Sorapuru....................................... 139
Stuffed Peppers With Shrimp Mrs. Evelyn Wismar 139
Deviled Crabs Mrs. Daisy Young.. 140
Ground Beef Casserole Mrs. Daisy Young 140

SOUL

Red Beans And Rice Dr. Ruby Broadway 141
Chili (Hartman Style) Mrs. Marguerite H. Rucker........................... 141
Gumbo – Bologna Style Mr. Clarence Holmes 142
Sweet Potatoes W/ Glaze Ms. Myrna Thompson 143

SOUTHWESTERN

Texas Chili Mr. W. Timothy Beckett... 144
It's Not Exactly Macaroni and Cheese Dr. Allan Burkett.................. 144
Monique's Chili Monica D. Courvertier.. 145
Chili Mrs. Susan Sergeant 145

NATIVE AMERICAN

Succotash Mrs. Sylvia Norman Oliver And Mrs. Shirley L. Alvis 146

CARIBBEAN

Robert's Puerto Rican Hot Tamales Mrs. Monica Couvertier 146

EUROPEAN

Pheasant Pot Pie Dr. Gerald Payton And Dr. Sharon Payton 147
....
Quiche Lorraine Mrs. Helen W. Beckett 147
Pork and Saurekraut Dr. Ellen Merrill 148
German Potato Salad Mrs. Blanche Cook 149
German Springerle Cookies Dr. Keith M. Wismar 149

BREADS/PASTRIES/CAKES

Carrot Cake Aisha El-Amin 150
Fruit Cake Mrs. Helen W. Beckett 150
Monkey Bread Mrs. Sylvia F. Cook 151
Okie Chocolate Cake Ms. Florence Lyons 151
Lussekatter (Swedish Letter Buns) Mrs. Helen Malin 152
Viennese Torte Mrs. Helen Malin 153
Apple Brown Betty with Hard Sauce Linda G. Nash 154
Pecan Pie Ms. Beryl Segre 154
Sweet Potato Pie Delight Mrs. Debra Surtain 155
Larry's Munchy Pecan Pie Lawrence R. Williams Sr. 155
Pecan Brittle Mrs. Daisy Young 155
Cream Puffs Mrs. Daisy Young 156
Creole Calas Dr. Jacqueline G. Houston 156
Million Dollar Chocolate Cake Mrs. Marie Wiggan Houston 157

FAIR DILLARD:
A COLLECTION OF CONTEMPORARY RECIPES

NEW ORLEANS

Chef Joynell's Crawfish Bread Dillard Dining Services 161
Daube Glacé Mrs. Leah Chase & Edgar "Dook" Chase Iv 162
Oyster Patties Zella Palmer 163
Oyster Loaf Zella Palmer 163
Rotel Dip Zella Palmer 164
Creole Tomato Dressing Zella Palmer 164
Seafood Gumbo Zella Palmer 165
Grillades Zella Palmer 166
Shrimp Creole Zella Palmer 167

Louisiana Pepper Jelly Sweet and Spicy Wings Zella Palmer.........167
Veal Panee (Breaded Veal) Zella Palmer 168
New Orleans Barbecue Shrimp Zella Palmer..............................168
Sauteed Deer Tenderloins Anthony Bennett..............................169
Chargrilled Oysters Miss Linda Green "Yakamein Lady" 169
Stuffed Veal Pocket with Oyster Dressing Miss Linda Green 170
Smothered Turkey Necks and Rice Miss Linda Green 170
Red Beans and Rice Miss Linda Green..................................171
Stuffed Bell Peppers Miss Linda Green................................172
Cornbread Mary Louise Thomas 172
Crawfish Bisque Mary Louise Thomas 173
Jambalaya Mary Louise Thomas 174
Redfish Courtbouillon Mary Louise Thomas 175
Oyster and Artichoke Soup Beverly Mckenna 176
Thanksgiving Leftover Turkey Bone Gumbo Liz Williams 176
Lake Charles Oxtail & Grits Chef Lyle Broussard 177
Crawfish Etouffee-Mamou Style Donna Reed Harper 177
Aunt Lucille's Stuffed Crabs Kemberley Washington 178
Grandma Annie's Smothered Okra & Shrimp Jon Renthrope...........179
Creole Jambalaya Ms. Sybil Haydel Morial.............................180
My Mother's Creole White Beans Ms. Sybil Haydel Morial.............180
Gran's Filè Gumbo Ms. Sybil Haydel Morial............................181
Queen Reesie's Stuffed Mirlitons Cherice Harrison-Nelson.............182
Shrimp Stew Mrs. Sandra Peychaud Dalcour............................182

AMERICAN

Roasted Pumpkin Soup Chef Kevin Mitchell 183
Southside Beef Chili Mrs. Bertha Glinsey............................184

SOUTHERN

Charleston Okra Soup Chef Benjamin Dennis 185
Sauteed Shrimp Cakes Chef Joseph G. Randall 185
Slowcooked Butterbeans & Okra Dr. Howard Jason Conyers............186
Hoppin John Audrey Vice...187

INTERNATIONAL

Koshary Dr. Abdullah Darwish..188
Black-Eyed Peas Hummus with Chili Paste Chef Pierre Thiam........189
Cowpeas (Mpindi/Kunde) Edie Mukiibi 190
Jollof Rice Chef Tunde Wey 190
Darlene Delicious Curry Chicken Darlene A. Moore....................191
Doro Wat (Ethiopian Chicken) Dr. Wodajo Welldaregay................192
Kolkata India Vegetable Croquettes Dr. Julie Basu-Ray 193
Cuban Chicken Soup Zella Palmer 194

Puerto Rican Creole Lasagna Zella Palmer 194
Tuscan White Bean Soup Donna Cummings 195
Mexican Crawfish Cornbread Dr. Yolanda W. Page.......................... 195

VEGETARIAN

Oven Roasted Okra Chef Gason Nelson.. 196
Cornbread with Cheese and Chiles Toni Tipton-Martin 196
Black Bean And Spinach Enchiladas M. Shannon Williamson 197
Roasted Almonds Julia Turshen 198

DESSERTS

Oreo Cheesecake Mrs. Adria N. Kimbrough, Esq. 199
Quick Italian Cream Cake Mrs. Adria N. Kimbrough, Esq. 200
Oatmeal Chocolate Chip Cookies Mrs. Marjorie L. Kimbrough........... 201
Mrs. Glinsey's Lemon Supreme Cake Bertha Glinsey 201
Southern Pecan Cheesecake Zella Palmer 202
Key Lime Cake Mrs. Adria N. Kimbrough, Esq. 202
Madame Barbara Trevigne Belle Calas Madame Barbara Trevigne . 203
Honey Bread Pudding V. Sheree Williams.. 204
Old Fashioned Pineapple Sherbert Gisele Perez 204
Fresh Strawberry Shortbread Mary Louise Thomas 205
Banana Macadamia Nut Bread Dr. Yolanda W. Page 205
Hucklebucks Dr. Mona Lisa Saloy 206

BEVERAGES

Bleu Devil Colada Michelle M. Mathews 207
Amaretto Punch M. Shannon Williamson. 208
Brazilian Lemonade Zella Palmer.. 208
Strawberry Basil Lemonade Zella Palmer 209
Grandmother Catherine's Kentucky Eggnog Dr. Alice J. Palmer 209